THE BROKEN STRING

An integrated approach to southern African HISTORY

Recommended for Standard 6/7

Emilia Potenza

with Ruth Versfeld as methodology adviser

Maskew Miller Longman

Some of the other titles in this series:

Hands-on History: An integrated approach to South African History;
(Standard 5 - 6) by **Emilia Potenza** *and* **Diane Favis**

World Alive: An integrated approach to Biology;
(Standard 5 - 6) by **Mark Potterton**

Get the Message: An integrated approach to English and the Media;
(Standard 5 - 6) by **Emilia Potenza**

Get the Picture! An integrated approach to English and the Media;
(Standard 6 - 7) by **Peter Ranby**

Going Places: An integrated approach to Geography;
(Standard 6 - 7) by **Peter Ranby**

In conceptualising this book, I benefited greatly from discussions with Professor John Parkington, Sally von Holdt, David Hiscock, Nigel Penn, Barbara Johannesson, Candy Malherbe, Clive Dyer and Stephen Rothenburg.

I am also grateful to Professor Allan Morris, Professor Martin Hall, Professor Revil Mason, and Rob Siebörger for their comments on sections of the manuscript.

Some of the material in **The Broken String** is based on ideas that were workshopped at Sacred Heart College. Thanks to Diane Favis, John McCormick and Tom Waspe for their contribution to the developing and testing of this book.

A special thanks to Ruth Versfeld for her encouragement and good ideas. Thanks also to Mary Monteith and Peter Ranby who worked with me on a regular basis throughout the difficult months of writing.

And finally, to Lorna Marshall, whose work inspired much of this book.

We are indebted to Misereor, Germany, for its generous donation which has made this project possible.

Emilia Potenza

Maskew Miller Longman (Pty) Ltd
Howard Drive, Pinelands, Cape Town

Offices in Johannesburg, Durban, Port Elizabeth, Kimberley, King William's Town, Pietersburg, Nelspruit, Umtata and Mafikeng and representatives throughout southern Africa.

Copyright © Sacred Heart College and Catholic Institute of Education 1992

First Edition 1992
Third Impression 1995

ISBN 0 636 01919 5

Cover photographs by Paul Weinberg, SouthLight
Cover design and illustration by Jeff Rankin, Clear Pictures
Illustrated by Danielle Woolf, Heather Davidson and Justin Wells
Printed by Creda Press
Eliot Avenue, Eppindust II

FOREWORD

For many years it was widely believed that the only reliable form of knowledge was the written word. Books, diaries, documents, newspapers — these all commanded respect because their words could be preserved. Yet we now know that even the printed word can be misleading. For example, certain history books taught, inaccurately, that Africans arrived in southern Africa at more or less the same time as European settlers landed in the Cape. Some books emphasised differences amongst people. And while most text books acknowledged that the Khoisan had lived in South Africa for a very long time, the writers saw them as 'primitive', and paid very little respect to their history.

When European settlers arrived in South Africa, most of them could read and write. They rightly valued the written word as a precious form of knowledge. But European scholars made the mistake of thinking that writing was the only way that knowledge could be passed on. Where they did not find books in Africa, they simply assumed that Africa had no history.

The Broken String shows us how wrong they were! This book brings to us just a taste of Africa's rich heritage which existed long before colonial times. In this book, we learn about South Africa's distant past not only through the written word, but through many other forms of evidence — from human remains, pottery, tools, rock paintings and buildings, as well as from our cultural traditions and the stories and memories passed on to us by our elders.

The Broken String presents this wealth of knowledge in a richly visual, well-informed and challenging way. By giving voice to the stories and experiences of the people themselves, this book encourages the student to be sensitive to those people of the past, and to try to understand their lives, their needs and their problems. It teaches the student how to interact with this information, to actually take part in exploring new knowledge. Perhaps most important, *The Broken String* leads the mind to think independently, and to break out of the old habits of judging and labelling people.

For, in spite of the many interesting differences which exist amongst us today, we all share a strong and exciting heritage. We all belong to the same family of human beings. It is this understanding, which the past can teach us, that will help us to work towards a future South Africa in which all our voices will be heard, and respected.

Luli Callinicos

CONTENTS

Page

To the Student vii

Unit 1: THE ORIGIN OF PEOPLE 1

Unit 2:
ARCHAEOLOGY — A WAY OF REDISCOVERING THE PAST
Evidence of human settlement in southern Africa to AD 1500 ... 9

Unit 3: HUNTER-GATHERERS IN SOUTHERN AFRICA
Case study on the !Kung 21

Unit 4: THE ARRIVAL OF THE KHOIKHOI
Herding people come south 45

Unit 5: AFRICAN FARMERS IN SOUTHERN AFRICA
The first farmers come to settle 59

Unit 6: THE STRUGGLE OVER LAND:
Khoikhoi meet Dutch 75

Unit 7: THE STRUGGLE OVER LAND:
The Northern Frontier 89

Unit 8: THE STRUGGLE OVER LAND:
The Basotho lose out 109

Unit 9: WE WHO WERE FIRST, HAVE COME TO BE LAST
Changes experienced by the !Kung in the last 40 years ... 127

Bibliography 143
Acknowledgements 146

SAN

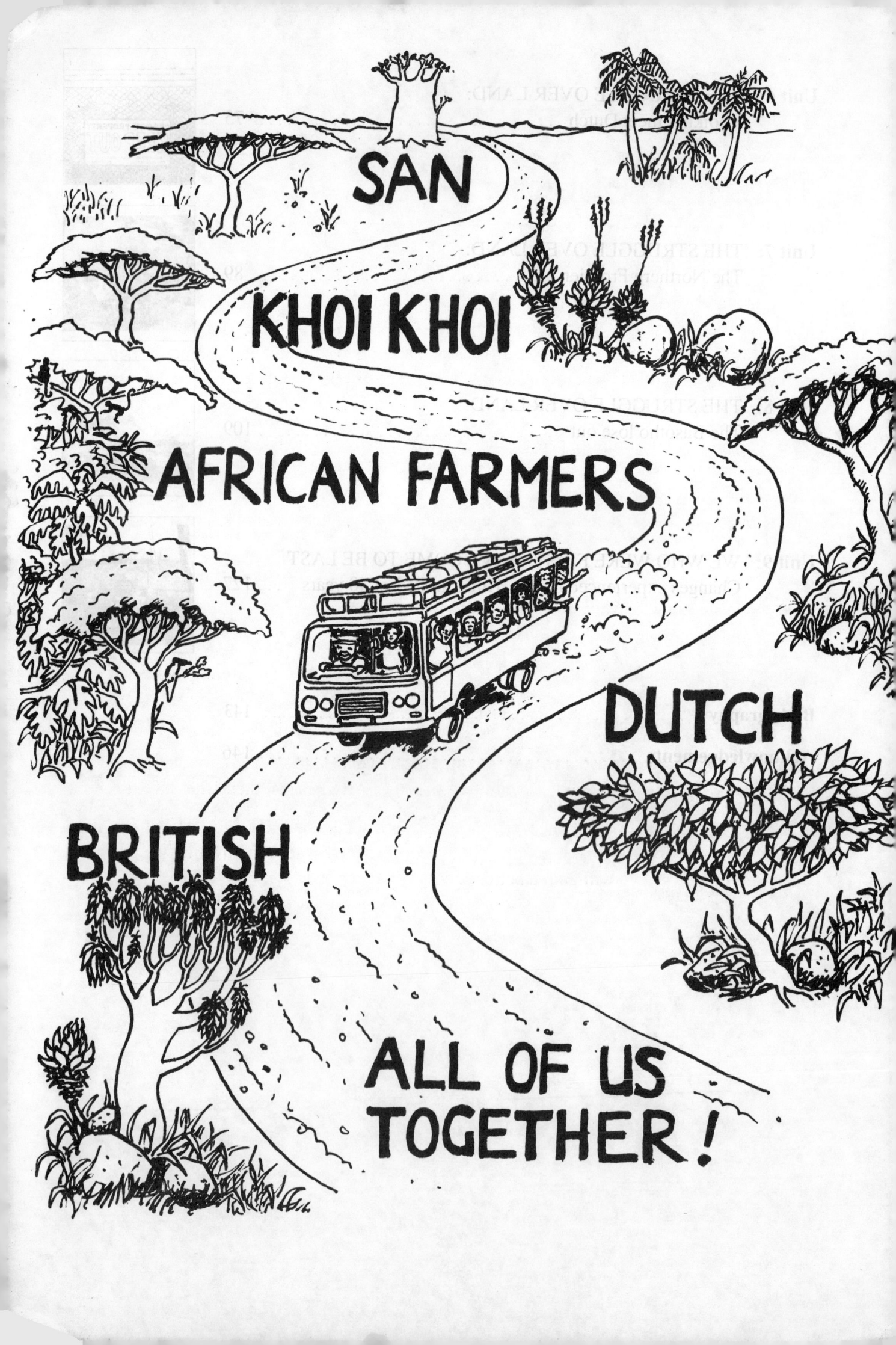

KHOI KHOI

AFRICAN FARMERS

DUTCH

BRITISH

ALL OF US TOGETHER!

TO THE STUDENT

You are about to go on an unusual journey into the past.

To understand what is happening in our country today means travelling right back to nearly 100 000 years ago. We will meet the first people like ourselves **in the world**, who appeared on South African soil. They were the ancestors of the San or Bushmen. They were nomads, who lived by hunting and gathering. This is how people have lived all over the world for most of human history.

Next we will meet the herding peoples who called themselves the Khoikhoi. Then come the first farmers. We will discover that there was trade and contact between all these groups, as well as some conflict over land and animals. But, the country was large enough for the San, the Khoikhoi and these African farmers to live their lives in relative peace.

After this, we will see the big changes that took place much later when the Dutch and then the British arrived. They began to trade with the people of South Africa. For some time, no one group was in control. But, as the number of people increased, the competition for the land became greater.

A long, drawn-out struggle over land began in the 18th Century. Different groups had different ideas about who owned the land and how it should be used. As a result, there were many conflicts leading to bitter wars in which many people died.

Finally, we will notice how the British and the Boers managed to gain control over most of the country. This meant that large numbers of South Africans lost their land.

Many of the people that we will meet on this journey are not famous. They are the ordinary men, women and children of our country. By listening to their voices and by thinking and seeing for ourselves, we will gain a better understanding of our country's history.

People have broken the string
for me
Therefore, the place became
like this to me
The place does not feel to me
as the place used to feel
The place does not feel pleasant to me
because the string has broken for me.

Adapted from a **San poem**

UNIT 1

The origin of people

UNIT 1

The origin of people

People are the most complex creatures on earth. There are many aspects of our behaviour that make us quite different from other animals. What makes us so special? In what ways do we differ from other animals? Let's look at some of the differences.

Exercise 1

1. With a partner, list all the things you do that other animals don't.

    One of the things that makes us different from all other animals is that we wonder about things i.e. we try to **make sense of the world we live in**. For example, we wonder about where we come from. We want to know about our ancestors and what life was like in the past.

    [Cartoon: A father says "OH RITA STOP STARING INTO SPACE AND DO SOMETHING CONSTRUCTIVE. GET ON WITH YOUR HOMEWORK." Rita replies "Do you mind Dad? I'm just doing a bit of wondering. That's supposed to make me different from other animals. When last did you wonder?"]

2. Write down some of the things you wonder about. Discuss any two of these with your partner.

Skeletons in our cupboards

Have you heard the expression we use to talk about the things in our past that we don't want people to know about — "skeletons in our cupboards"? Have you ever been told weird and wonderful stories about what one or other of your relatives did in the past? Some of these stories may be hard to believe. They may even be too embarrassing to repeat.

Exercise 2

1. Try to remember an interesting story that you have been told about a member of your family. Choose a story that gives some idea of what life must have been like at the time. Or what about a story that has had a big effect on the way your life has turned out?

2. Write down a few points to remind yourself of the story. Then tell your story to one of your classmates.

Who told you this story? Will you tell your children? This is oral history.

UNIT 1

Our old people are our libraries.

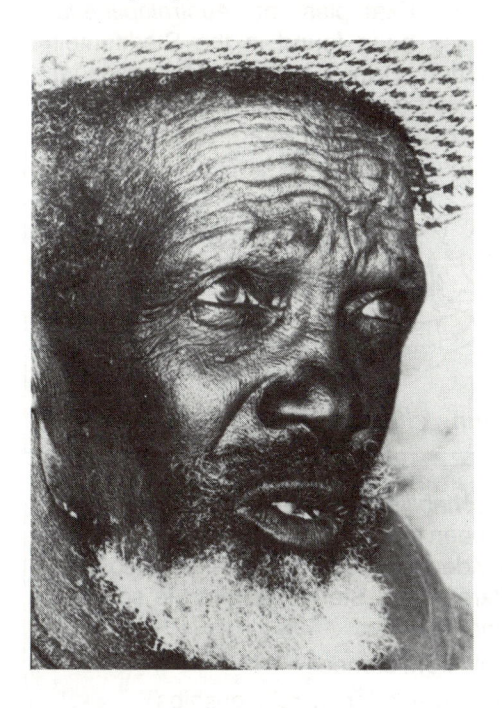

"Time past
Lights up today
And tomorrow,
Making it clear."

Antonio Mussapi

The human family — some fascinating facts

And now for the dramatic story that explains how we turned out to be the way we are — well at least physically. Most scholars agree that the human family started in Africa and that the oldest skeletons of creatures like ourselves have been found in South Africa!

Our earliest known ancestor, *Australopithecus afarensis*, lived four million years ago. Some of the oldest examples of this creature are fossils* found at Hadar in Ethiopia. They
- did not have stone tools
- weighed about 50 kgs
- walked upright on two legs.

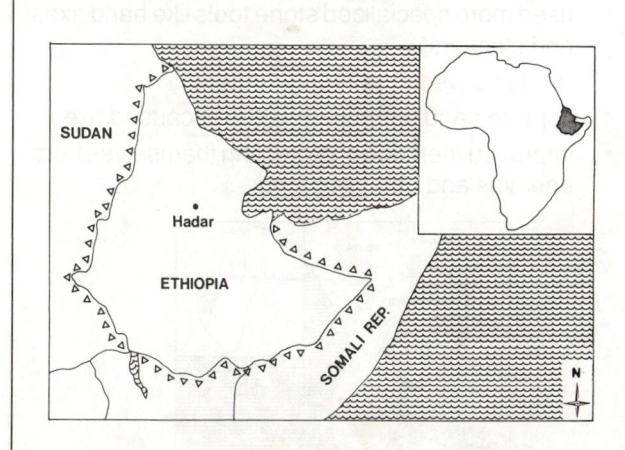

Australopithecus afarensis

3

UNIT 1

Another example of this species — *Australopithecus africanus* — was found at Taung in the northern Cape by Professor Raymond Dart. The Taung skull was 3 million years old. Examples of *Australopithecus africanus* have also been found in the Sterkfontein Caves in the southern Transvaal and at Makapansgat. The most famous of these fossils, a female skull dating between three and one million years ago, has been nicknamed "Mrs Ples".

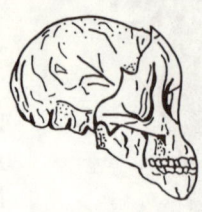

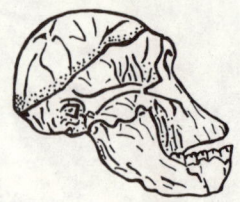

Australopithecus africanus   *The Taung child*   *"Mrs Ples"*

Did you know? The extent of family among baboons is the relationship between a mother and her offspring. Males do not recognise their offspring.

Fossils of *Homo habilis* that date back to two million years ago have been found at Lake Turkana in northern Kenya. Other evidence of *Homo habilis* has also been found at Swartkrans and Sterkfontein in the southern Transvaal. *Homo habilis*
- made tools from stones
- started to develop family relationships
- constructed stone walls for shelter.

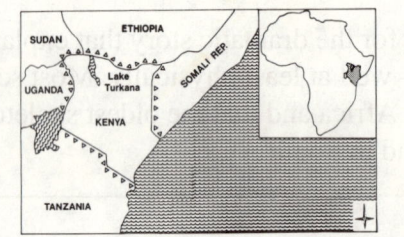

Homo habilis

About 1,5 million years ago, a more advanced being appeared. It had a bigger brain than *habilis* and became known as *Homo erectus* or upright human. Specimens of *Homo erectus* have been found just south of Rabat in Morocco, at Olduvai Gorge in Tanzania and at Swartkrans in South Africa. *Homo erectus*
- used more specialized stone tools like hand axes and cleavers*
- lived in caves
- captured and controlled naturally caused **fire**
- improved methods of protecting themselves from enemies and obtaining food.

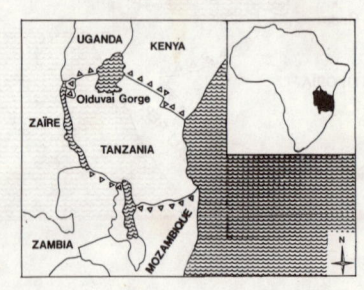

Homo erectus

4

UNIT 1

Homo sapiens may well have originated in South Africa. About 300 000 years ago, we begin to find beings who are more like ourselves. One example was found near Saldanha in the western Cape. The skull cap found there is enough to show the beginnings of physical characteristics of people as we know them today.

'Saldanha' skull

Homo sapiens

The oldest skeletons of people like ourselves, what we now call anatomically modern people, also known as *Homo sapiens sapiens*, date to around 100 000 years ago. Their remains have been found at Klasies River Mouth near Storms River in the Cape and at Border Cave on the border between Natal and Swaziland.

Anatomically modern people
- used smaller, more delicate tools which showed increasing development of skills
- had the use of fire
- had more highly-developed family relationships
- held ceremonies for burying the dead and had some form of religious belief.

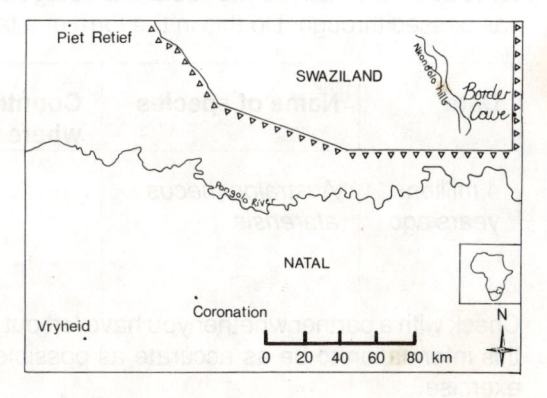

Homo sapiens sapiens

New words

- fossil — part or imprint of ancient plant or animal once buried in the earth, now hardened like rock.
- cleaver — very sharp stone tool that could be used as a knife.

UNIT 1

Something to think about

Bones of two larger kinds of *Australopithecines*, dating from about 2 million to 1,5 million years ago, have been found in both East and South Africa. These creatures, known as *Australopithecus robustus* and *Australophithecus boisei,* lived at the same time as *Homo habilis*. However, most scientists believe that they are a sideline of human evolution and that they eventually became extinct without leaving any descendants.

Another sideline of human evolution appeared later. This species became known as *Homo sapiens neanderthalensis* or "Neanderthal Man". It lived from about 75 000 to 35 000 years ago in Europe and those parts of Africa and Asia that border on the Mediterranean Sea. It became extinct at about the same time as modern people appeared on the scene. We do not yet know the reason for this.

Australopithecus robustus

Take note!

It is a good idea to take notes when you are presented with important factual information that you are expected to remember. There are different ways of taking notes. In the next exercise you will practise making notes of the information you have just read — **in the form of a table**.

Exercise 3

Write down the main points about each stage of development that the human family has passed through. Do this in the form of a table:

Date	Name of species	Country and area where found	~~One~~ important characteristic~~s~~
4 million years ago	*Australopithecus afarensis*		

Check with a partner whether you have left out any important information. You need this information to be as accurate as possible because you will use it in the next exercise.

Africa — The cradle of humanity

It is not difficult to see why Africa is sometimes referred to as the cradle of humanity. The reasons become very clear when we see, altogether on one map, some of the evidence of forms of human life that have been found in Africa.

UNIT 1

Exercise 4

This is a mapping activity for which you will need an atlas. Make sure you follow each stage of this exercise carefully.

1. Trace a map of Africa from an atlas or draw a freehand outline. Try to make it as big as your piece of paper will allow.

2. Now fill in all the **countries** where remains of early forms of the human family have been found. Refer to the table you did in Exercise 3. Try to be as neat and accurate as possible.

3. The next step involves filling in the names of **cities** and **towns** and other areas like gorges and lakes that you listed in your table. The little maps provided in the table **The human family — some fascinating facts**, as well as information from an atlas, should help you to do this correctly.

    Maps have not been provided to show places that are in South Africa — except for Border Cave. You should be able to find out where these places are with the help of an atlas.
    Note: The place names on these maps are relatively modern and were not used in ancient times.

4. Now include a small drawing on your map of something that shows an important characteristic of each stage of development. Once again, use the summarised information from your table to help you. You may choose to draw an object, a place of shelter, a family scene or even a grave. Draw a box around this. Make sure that one corner of the box touches the dot that shows the town or the physical feature where the discovery was made.

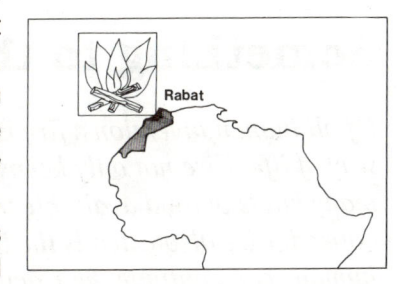

5. Next, provide a key at the bottom of your map to show the five different stages of development that the human family has passed through. Use a different colour for each stage. Next to each square of your key, write the name of the species and how long ago they appeared e.g. Purple — *Homo erectus* approximately 1,5 million years ago.

6. Finally, shade each section of your map where evidence has been found of a particular species in the colour which matches your key. This will make it easy for anybody looking at your map to see where our different ancestors lived and how long ago they roamed Africa.

How accurate is your map?

The following exercise provides a way for you to test how accurate your map is.

Exercise 5

1. See whether you can fill in the information that has been left out of this timeline by using only your map as a reference. Don't look back to the table of information or to your summarised notes of it.

UNIT 1

Copy the timeline onto a piece of paper and fill in the missing information for questions 1-6.

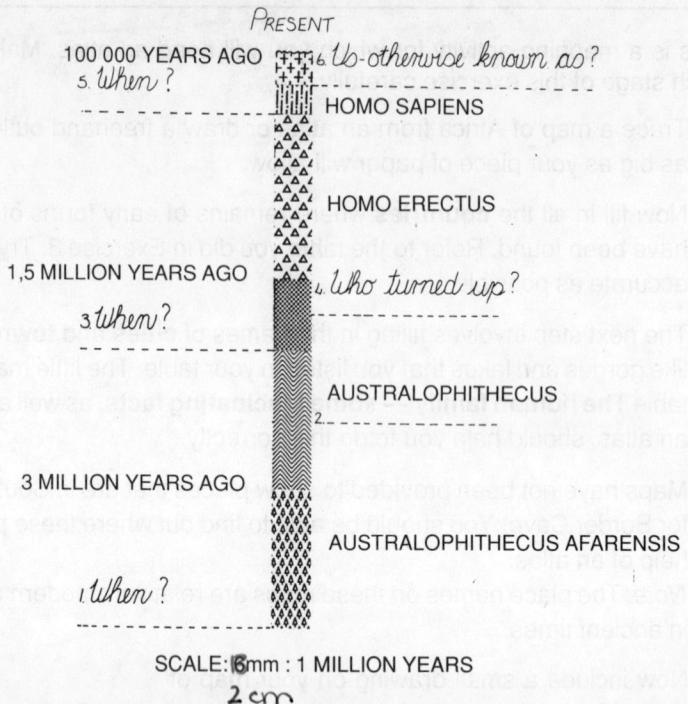

```
                              PRESENT
    100 000 YEARS AGO ──── 6. Us-otherwise known as?
    5. When? ─────────────
                              HOMO SAPIENS

                              HOMO ERECTUS

    1,5 MILLION YEARS AGO ─── 4. Who turned up?
    3. When? ─────────────
                              AUSTRALOPITHECUS
                          2. ─────────────────
    3 MILLION YEARS AGO

                              AUSTRALOPITHECUS AFARENSIS
    1. When? ─────────────

            SCALE: 6mm : 1 MILLION YEARS
                   2 cm
```

Something to think about

Of all human inventions, fire is the one that has had the greatest impact on our way of life. Fire not only keeps us warm, but it also cooks our meals and makes many kinds of food available to us that are impossible to chew or digest unless cooked. Fire also extends the length of our day. With the light provided by fire, humans can continue their activities well into the night. Perhaps the **Homo erectus** *people, sitting around their fires at night, recounted the stories of their history and planned their activities for the next day.*

from **Four Million Years of Hominid Evolution**, Stream Educational Movement

Summing up

In this unit you learned about the following ideas:

1. Oral history is a way of recording the past.

2. Africa is known as "the cradle of humanity" because so many examples of different forms of human life have been found here.

3. To date, the oldest evidence of human beings (anatomically modern people) has been found in South Africa.

People like ourselves have been living in South Africa for about 100 000 years. In the next unit, you will study some of the remains or evidence of their lives from about 100 000 years ago until AD 1500.

8

UNIT 2

Archaeology — A way of rediscovering the past

UNIT 2

Archaeology — A way of rediscovering the past

How do we find out about the past? For recent events that we were personally involved in, we rely on our memories. To know about events earlier than this, we have to ask elderly relatives and friends to recall their experiences of that time. We can also read books or see films about the past.

But, how do the writers of these books and the makers of the films find out about thousands or even millions of years ago — about times that have become forgotten to living memory, and of which there are no written records? How, for example, have we come to know all this fascinating information about the origin of people?

The distant past can be studied by means of archaeology. Archaeologists try to find the answers to certain questions about people in the past. To do this they look for evidence of the people they are interested in. This means looking for places or sites where people lived and left behind remains.

Archaeology is the study of past people's behaviour from their material remains.

It is almost impossible for people who have spent some time at a place not to leave evidence of their passing. Paths, flattened sleeping spots, fireplaces and other remains, including rubbish, can give us many clues about the people who were there and their activities.

Digging in dustbins

You would be surprised at how much history you can find in a dustbin.

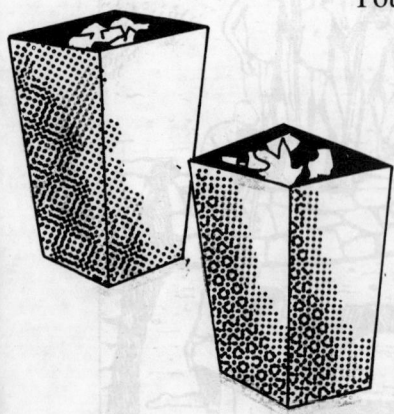

Exercise 1

Get hold of the dustbins from various rooms of your school e.g. an office, classroom, laboratory or even the staffroom! Examine the contents carefully.

1. List the contents of the bins.

2. What do the contents of the bins tell you about
   a. the kinds of activities that take place in these rooms?
   b. the people who are involved in these activities?

UNIT 2

> LOOK! I FOUND THIS WINE BOTTLE IN THE STAFFROOM BIN!

> SO! THAT'S WHAT TEACHERS GET UP TO, IS IT?

Exercise 2

The following items were found in the dustbin of the Zotwana family, starting from the top and working towards the bottom:

some chicken bones
carrot peelings
a *New Nation* newspaper
2 empty Stoney cans
4 cigarette butts
1 Jungle Oats box
many egg shells
4 penlite batteries
1 empty Finesse hair shampoo bottle
potato peels
mutton bones
an empty Dogmor packet
3 empty Checkers bags
a *Family Radio and TV* magazine
many tea bags
a milk carton

UNIT 2

1. Use these "clues" to work out as much as possible about this family. Write down your ideas in a paragraph of about 10 – 15 lines.

> **HOW TO STRUCTURE YOUR PARAGRAPH**
> - Start with a main idea or topic sentence which sums up what the whole paragraph is going to be about.
> - Develop your paragraph by selecting four or five items from the dustbin and explaining what each item tells you about the family.

2. Work out roughly the order in which different activities took place. How do you know this?

Exercise 3

Discuss these questions in pairs.

1. Has any member of this family drunk coffee in the last day or two?
2. What other activities could this family have been involved in for which there is no evidence?
3. What limits archaeologists in their attempts to reconstruct the past?

Rubbish can be precious

Rubbish and other remains are considered precious by archaeologists. Archaeologists carefully dig up the rubbish and other remains left behind by people living many thousands of years ago. This includes things like the fossils of plants, skeletons of animals as well as stone or metal objects. They know that, in almost all cases, the oldest material will be at the bottom and the most recent on top.

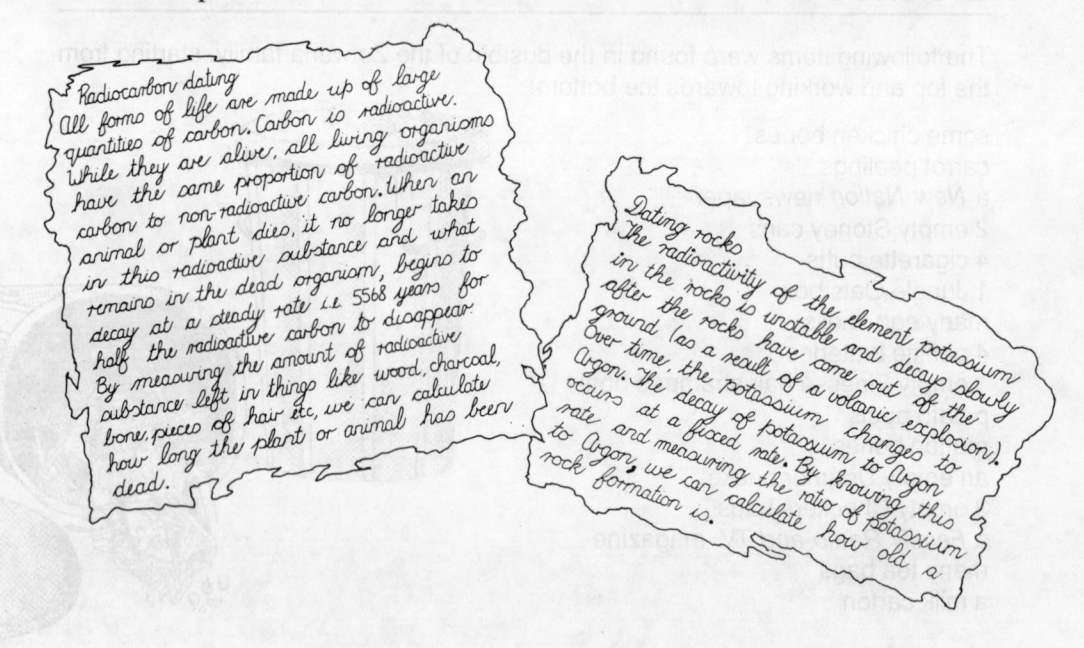

Radiocarbon dating
All forms of life are made up of large quantities of carbon. Carbon is radioactive. While they are alive, all living organisms have the same proportion of radioactive carbon to non-radioactive carbon. When an animal or plant dies, it no longer takes in this radioactive substance and what remains in the dead organism, begins to decay at a steady rate i.e. 5568 years for half the radioactive carbon to disappear. By measuring the amount of radioactive substance left in things like wood, charcoal, bone, pieces of hair etc, we can calculate how long the plant or animal has been dead.

Dating rocks
The radioactivity of the element potassium in the rocks is unstable and decays slowly after the rocks have come out of the ground (as a result of a volcanic explosion). Over time, the potassium changes to Argon. The decay of potassium to Argon occurs at a fixed rate. By knowing this rate and measuring the ratio of potassium to Argon, we can calculate how old a rock formation is.

12

Things which have been left exactly where people dropped them are said to be in "primary context". By making maps of the material left on a site, archaeologists can suggest how different people used their living space e.g. where they slept, cooked and made tools. Sometimes it is possible to work out what people ate, how they adapted to their environment, how they treated each other and even what they believed in.

A Tswana family gather at the burial of a 14 year old girl.

Over 250 years later archaeologists discover the skeleton of the same girl.

Everyone in society creates rubbish, builds shelters and uses tools which may survive through time. So, archaeology can tell us as much about ordinary people as about rulers or famous people and as much about everyday life as about great events.

Archaeologists, like other people who study the past, select information which helps them to answer the questions about the past they believe are important. Different archaeologists ask different questions about the past. Our knowledge of history grows and broadens as more archaeologists ask new questions and find new answers.

Evidence of human settlement in southern Africa

Archaeological evidence shows that southern Africa has one of the longest records of human activity anywhere in the world. Yet, until very recently, school students in South Africa only learnt the history of the last few hundred years.

This was because school histories about South Africa generally relied on written documents. Most of these documents tell us about the spread of

UNIT 2

European settlement around the world dating from about AD 1500. By concentrating on these documents, school histories have often left out fascinating information about the history of this country before the arrival of the European settlers.

As we have seen, the full story begins millions of years ago — but it has to be told mainly by archaeologists. Archaeologists are able to provide us with information about the various human societies that developed in South Africa over time. They have put together this story from the tools, buildings, rock paintings, iron and copper furnaces and other things that were made by people and that have been buried in the South African soil for thousands of years. We call these things the material remains or the **material culture** of the societies that lived here.

*The following is an extract from **In our own Image** by Judy Seidman, p9.*

Material culture

Every group of people lives surrounded by the things they have made. Look around you: nearly everything you see in the classroom was made by human beings. We find desks, chairs, books, blackboards, shoes and clothes, pens, pencils and paper; walls made out of brick, windows and doors. At home we keep pots and pans and stoves for preparing food, beds to sleep on, tables and shelves, and many other items. We use cars and aeroplanes and ships and trains for transport. We communicate with telephones, televisions, radios and printing presses. The list can go on endlessly. To make these things, we need factories, full of other machines. People also create works of art, such as sculpture, paintings, and musical instruments. We even change the land around us, plowing farms where there were forests, digging holes in the ground for mines, and building hills with the dirt taken out of these holes.

All of these products, or artifacts, together constitute our material culture.

Imagine an archaeologist digging up the ruins of a village that our ancestors had lived in, hundreds of years ago. He may find circles of stone, remaining from the houses that people lived in. (Such stone rings are found in Zimbabwe and parts of Botswana; the most impressive are found at Great Zimbabwe.) He may find pieces of clay pots, or even whole pots. He may find stone weapons, such as knives or arrow heads. He may find a sculpture of clay or metal. These are all remains of the material culture of the people who lived in that village. From those physical remains, the historian can attempt to put together a picture of how those people lived.

UNIT 2

A roadway of time for the people of southern Africa

Read the information in the table below about different stages of human development in southern Africa from about 1,5 million years ago. The material culture or artifacts that people made and left behind has helped archaeologists to put together a picture of how people lived. You will use this information in the exercise that follows later.

PERIOD OF HISTORY	MATERIAL CULTURE
EARLY STONE AGE	The earliest stone tools in southern Africa date to 1,5 million years ago. They were simple stones from which flakes were removed. These sharp-edged tools, or even the flakes that were chipped off, were used for cutting. Evidence of **Early Stone Age** communities shows that they lived mainly in caves near to rivers.
MIDDLE STONE AGE	In **Middle Stone Age** times, between about 150 000 to 30 000 years ago, people made long blade-like and triangular stone tools, some of which were probably used as spearheads. Middle Stone Age people along the coast ate shellfish from about 120 000 years ago. There is little evidence up to this time of the making of ornaments.
LATE STONE AGE	**Late Stone Age** tools appear about 30 000 years ago. These consist of smaller, finer tools — rounded scrapers, adzes* and segments which were put onto wooden handles. Later Stone Age people, like their ancestors, were hunter-gatherers who did not live in settled communities. They hunted with bows and poison-tipped arrows by about 14 000 years ago. There is a great deal of evidence of rock art, ornaments and burials with grave goods, such as shells and beads, like those used by the San* in more recent times. About 2 000 years ago, herders with domestic sheep and, later on, cattle arrived in the south-western Cape. They made tools out of pottery and bone, as well as stone tools but had no knowledge of iron smelting. They were the Khoikhoi* — the ancestors of the people the Europeans encountered when they reached the shores of southern Africa in 1488.
IRON AGE	About 1 800 years ago, **Iron Age** farmers who lived in more settled village communities, with crops, domestic animals, pottery and knowledge of smelting metals began spreading through southern Africa. Some Iron Age communities became wealthy states. These people were the ancestors of the modern-day Africans* of southern Africa. The Iron Age in southern Africa lasted until about 100 years ago.

UNIT 2

New words

- adzes — tools with a sharp edge for cutting or shaping wood.
- San — the name this book uses for the hunter-gatherer people of southern Africa from a few thousand years ago and their descendants. Some people refer to these people as Bushmen.
- Khoikhoi — a translation of a term that herding people gave to themselves and it probably means "proper people" or "men of men".
- Africans — black people in South Africa who speak Bantu languages. Your teacher will explain to you what the word Bantu means.

It is important to realise that the periods of history listed in the previous table describe a **way of life**. So it could happen that people followed different ways of life at the same time in different parts of the country eg a Stone Age way of life and an Iron Age one have existed alongside each other in certain areas. And over time, one or both of these ways of life would change.

Panic in the museum

Museums are usually quiet and orderly. You have to keep your voice down and pretend to be very interested in all the things on display. But, let's have a peep at what could be going on behind the scenes.

Exercise 4

Imagine that you are a cleaner in the South African Museum in Cape Town. You are dusting the inside of a display cabinet in the Archaeology section of the museum on a beautiful summer's day, whistling softly as a gentle breeze wafts through the room. Suddenly, the south-easter begins to blow and within seconds the breeze turns into a gale, lifting several precious bits of information out of the display cabinet into the air. You have the sense to dash over to the open window and close it and to gather up all the pieces of paper from the floor.

Then panic begins to set in. If you tell the person who supervises your section, you may well get fired. Your only option is to try to keep calm and see whether you can put all the information back in the right place again by yourself.

The display cabinet contained a map showing many places in southern Africa where remains have been found from the Early Stone Age until about AD 1500. You will find this map on the next two pages of this book. But, there are gaps where the information has blown away! All the bits of information that you picked up from the floor appear in the box below.

Your task is to work out where each bit of information belongs on the map. Don't write in your books. Either trace the map or work with a photocopy.

UNIT 2

This unusual head is one of several found at Lydenburg in 1962. It was made by Iron Age farmers in the sixth century AD.

This broken slab from Apollo 11 Cave was painted sometime between 19 000 and 27 000 years ago. It is the oldest dated rock art in Africa.

Iron Age stone walling found in the Transvaal and Orange Free State was used by modern-day Sotho-Tswana people to enclose cattle pens and courtyards around huts.

Sites in the south-western Cape have produced evidence of pointed-base pottery and domesticated sheep about 2000 years ago.

Early Stone Age tools like this hand axe were made several hundred thousand years ago. They were found throughout southern Africa.

One of the world's richest collections of Stone Age rock art is to be found in the Drakensberg Mountains. This collection includes many magnificent paintings such as this eland.

17

UNIT 2

MATERIAL CULTURE SHOWING THE EARLY HISTORY OF SOUTHERN AFRICA TO AD 1500

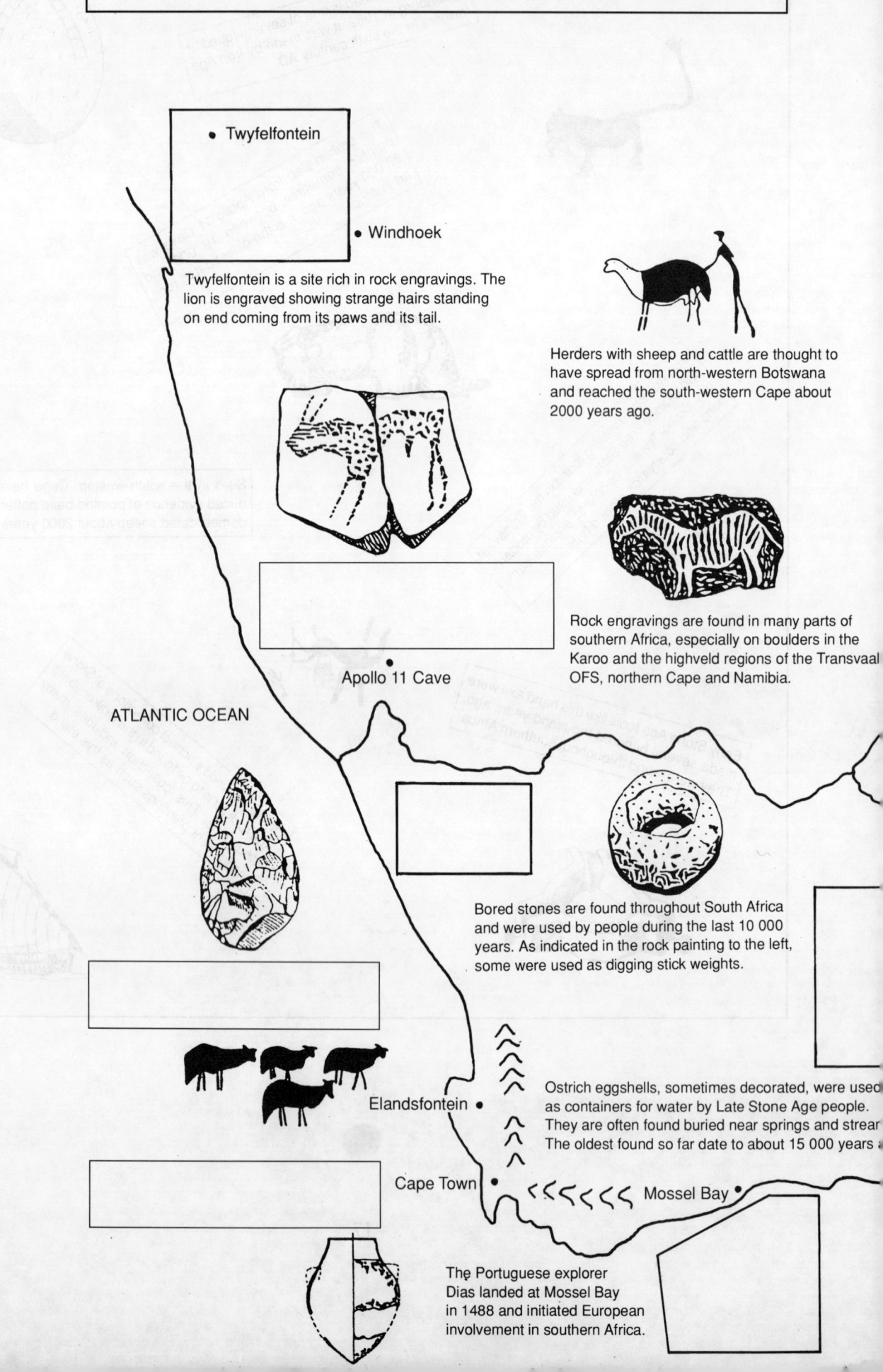

• Twyfelfontein

• Windhoek

Twyfelfontein is a site rich in rock engravings. The lion is engraved showing strange hairs standing on end coming from its paws and its tail.

Herders with sheep and cattle are thought to have spread from north-western Botswana and reached the south-western Cape about 2000 years ago.

Rock engravings are found in many parts of southern Africa, especially on boulders in the Karoo and the highveld regions of the Transvaal, OFS, northern Cape and Namibia.

• Apollo 11 Cave

ATLANTIC OCEAN

Bored stones are found throughout South Africa and were used by people during the last 10 000 years. As indicated in the rock painting to the left, some were used as digging stick weights.

Elandsfontein •

Ostrich eggshells, sometimes decorated, were used as containers for water by Late Stone Age people. They are often found buried near springs and streams. The oldest found so far date to about 15 000 years

Cape Town •   <<<<<<   Mossel Bay •

The Portuguese explorer Dias landed at Mossel Bay in 1488 and initiated European involvement in southern Africa.

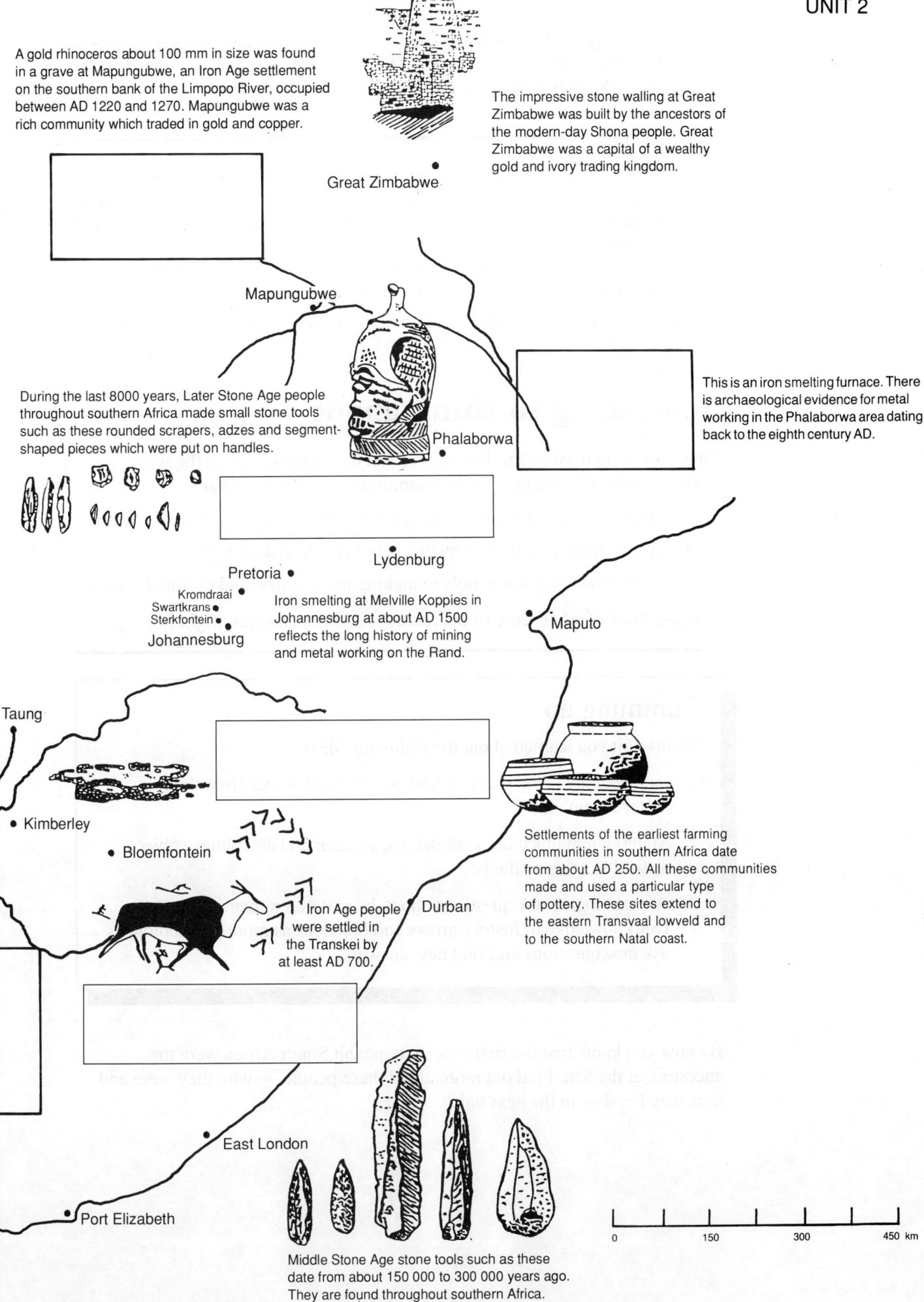

UNIT 2

A gold rhinoceros about 100 mm in size was found in a grave at Mapungubwe, an Iron Age settlement on the southern bank of the Limpopo River, occupied between AD 1220 and 1270. Mapungubwe was a rich community which traded in gold and copper.

The impressive stone walling at Great Zimbabwe was built by the ancestors of the modern-day Shona people. Great Zimbabwe was a capital of a wealthy gold and ivory trading kingdom.

• Great Zimbabwe

• Mapungubwe

During the last 8000 years, Later Stone Age people throughout southern Africa made small stone tools such as these rounded scrapers, adzes and segment-shaped pieces which were put on handles.

• Phalaborwa

This is an iron smelting furnace. There is archaeological evidence for metal working in the Phalaborwa area dating back to the eighth century AD.

• Pretoria   • Lydenburg
Kromdraai •
Swartkrans •
Sterkfontein •
Johannesburg

Iron smelting at Melville Koppies in Johannesburg at about AD 1500 reflects the long history of mining and metal working on the Rand.

• Maputo

• Taung

• Kimberley

• Bloemfontein

Iron Age people were settled in the Transkei by at least AD 700.

• Durban

Settlements of the earliest farming communities in southern Africa date from about AD 250. All these communities made and used a particular type of pottery. These sites extend to the eastern Transvaal lowveld and to the southern Natal coast.

• East London

• Port Elizabeth

0   150   300   450 km

Middle Stone Age stone tools such as these date from about 150 000 to 300 000 years ago. They are found throughout southern Africa.

UNIT 2

Once you have done this, shade all the evidence that has been included on the map in the colour that matches your key. This will show you at a glance what date has been put to many of the material objects found in southern Africa.

Exercise 5

Now that you've got yourself out of that tight spot, add a key to your map to highlight the **age** that each archaeological find belongs to. To do this, you need to use information from
- the table called **A Roadway of time for the people of southern Africa**
- the map for which you are making a key.

Decide on a different colour for each age e.g. Middle Stone Age — green. This key will be similar to the one you did in Unit 1.

Something to think about

There are many reasons for the changes that have taken place in the way human beings organise their lives. Examples of these changes are

- from capturing naturally caused fire to discovering how to make fire
- from a hunter-gatherer way of life to herding and farming
- from producing stone tools to making tools of iron and eventually steel.

Can you think of what some of the reasons for these changes might be?

Summing up

In this unit you learned about the following ideas:

1. Archaeology is the study of past people's behaviour from their material remains.

2. Material remains include skeletons, stone, metal and pottery objects, as well as other artifacts.

3. Archaeologists ask questions about the material remains they find. Our knowledge of history grows and broadens as more archaeologists ask new questions and find new answers.

By now you know that the first people to inhabit South Africa were the ancestors of the San. Find out more about these people — who they were and how they lived — in the next unit.

20

UNIT 3

Hunter-gatherers in southern Africa

UNIT 3

Hunter-gatherers in southern Africa

For more than 95% of the last 100 000 years, most people all over the world have followed a hunting and gathering way of life. Until recently, people living mostly by hunting and gathering could still be found in different parts of the world. But, over the last century, and particularly over the last thirty years, these communities have been forced to adopt a different way of life.

In the 1950s, several thousand San people were still hunting large game with poisoned arrows and gathering plant food in the Kalahari Desert in Namibia. One group, the !Kung, lived in an area called Nyae Nyae (pronounced ny ny, rhyming with high), near the border between Namibia and Botswana.

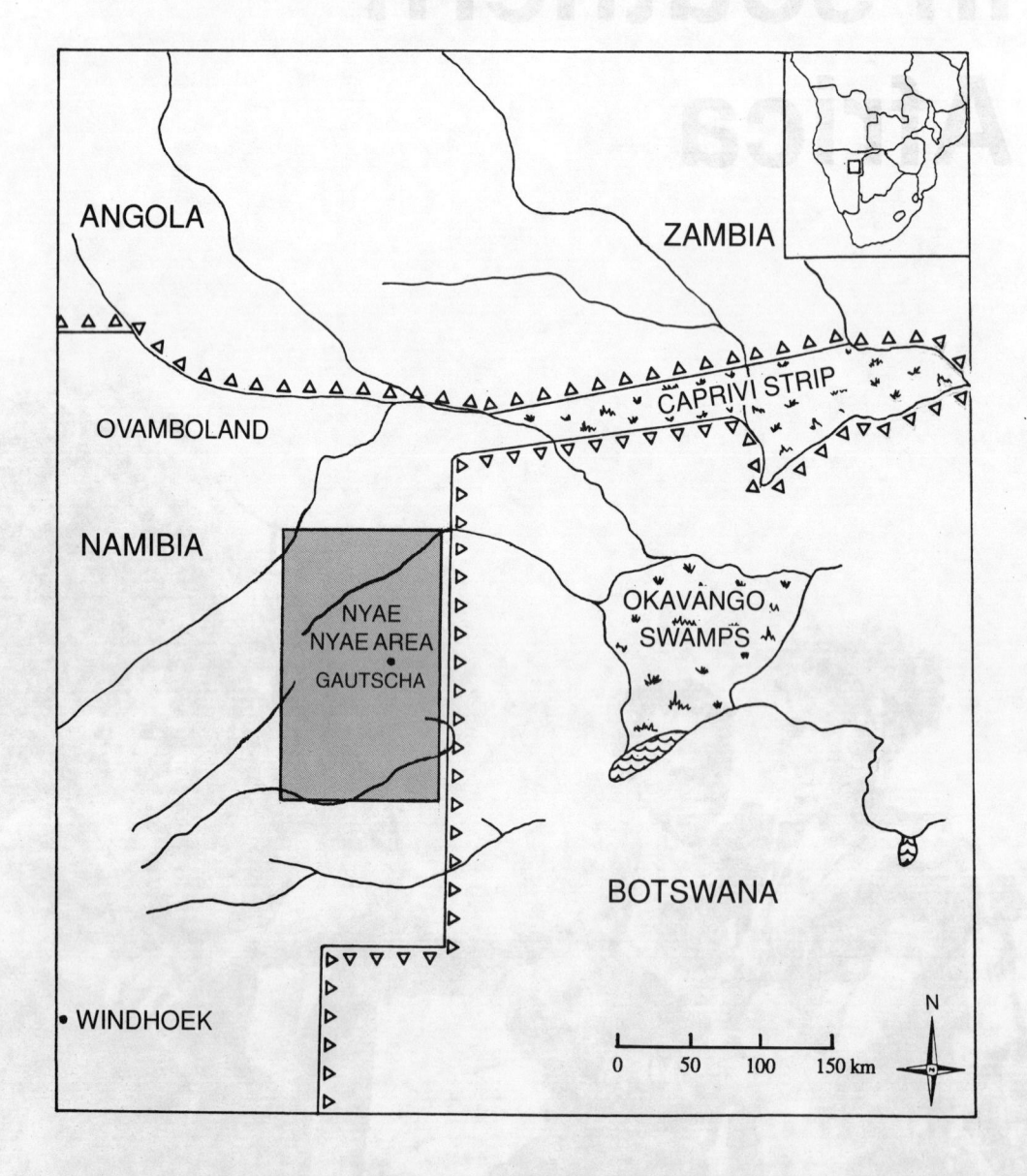

The !Kung were able to continue their ancient way of life largely because they lived in an area that was very difficult to reach. A stretch of land of about 200 kilometres, waterless for most of the year, lay between the closest farms and the Nyae Nyae area. Travelling across this area — even in trucks — was difficult: vehicles would get stuck in the sand, their tyres would get punctured or the seeds of the tall, dry grasses would clog up their radiators causing them to boil. These factors, for better or for worse, helped to protect the !Kung way of life from outside influences until about thirty years ago.

In the 1960s, the Department of Nature Conservation began to take over large sections of the traditional hunting lands of the Kalahari San for game and nature reserves. A law passed in 1970 meant that the !Kung lost 90% of their traditional land in Nyae Nyae. Today they have hardly any land on which to hunt and gather.

Although modern hunter-gatherers have changed and adapted to various influences over time, their lifestyle does offer clues to what a hunter-gatherer lifestyle must have been like in the distant past. How can we find out more about how the San, the last hunter-gatherers in southern Africa lived? After all, this is more or less how all human beings lived for hundreds of thousands of years.

A journey into the past

An American family, the Marshalls, spent several years living with the !Kung in Nyae Nyae in the 1950s. They studied their way of life in great detail and wrote books and made films about it. Their work has made it possible for us to get a very clear picture of what a hunting and gathering lifestyle was like for the !Kung.

Exercise 1

The Marshalls lived with some !Kung people. One of them was a woman called !U. Listen to the way !U might have described the !Kung way of life to the Marshalls. But remember that what she is saying applies to what life was probably like in the distant past and until the 1950s. Since then there have been many changes.

!U's speech has been divided into three parts to make it easier for you to follow. So, you will do this exercise in three parts.

1. Look at the photographs starting on page 25 that the Marshalls took as you listen to !U's words. Your teacher will read !U's words to you. What !U says will help you to work out what situation each photograph is showing. As you listen, note down some of the information that applies to each photograph on a separate sheet of paper.

2. Now use this information to write a caption for each photograph explaining clearly what it shows. Try to make your captions as interesting and original as possible.

    Each photograph has been numbered. Write down the number of each photograph on a piece of paper and then write a caption next to each one.

UNIT 3

!U's story

Part 1:

Our home is the Kalahari. We are the !Kung of Nyae Nyae. The Kalahari is a very big desert which takes up almost a third of southern Africa. Where we live, it is very dry. The big rains come in January, February and March but for the rest of the year, the rain never falls. During the season of the rain, water collects in pans. The largest of these is **Gautscha**. The happy people of **Gautscha** who live on the banks of the pan, delight in the water. Every day the children play in it, dancing and splashing and making patterns.

The land around us as far as you can see is very flat. There are no hills; nothing is higher than the termite hills and the baobab trees. For most of the year, we live without a roof. This means that you can always see the beauty of the morning, the setting sun and the blazing stars. The sky is also where our gods live and where the spirits of the dead move about.

"But don't you have houses?" you may be wondering. The answer to this question is that we don't have permanent dwellings. Although we return to the same waterholes, we don't reoccupy the old camp sites. We don't want to make new fires exactly where the old fires have been. To build new fires on the old sites might invite misfortune. Also, we don't like to tire out one spot of land.

Nobody owns the land and everybody has the right to use it. The place where we decide to settle is called our n!ore. Once we have decided where we will settle, the next act is to make a fire. This requires two fire sticks and a bunch of grass. Usually two men make fire together. As one pair of hands holds the bottom stick, the second pair is ready at the top to keep the twirling going. Making fire is the work of men and men carry their fire sticks with them constantly.

You can tell where a family has settled from its fire. The family hangs its possessions in the bushes near the fire, sits around the fire, cooks at it, sleeps at it. Fire, water and food hold our lives together. We have been so created. Without fire, we would have no light, no warmth; food could not be cooked. Even an old person can live by his fire. Someone will give him food and water and he will be warm.

Oh, we do have shelters. It is the woman's job to build a shelter. Often we women do not bother to build shelters unless it is raining. A woman can build a shelter in less than an hour — and, of course, the materials are always available all around us. We gather some slender branches from the bushes and push each branch into the ground. Then we bend their tops together and weave them into each other making the frame of the shelter. Next we bring armloads of tall grass which we pat into place over the frame, and the job is done!

"And what about clothes?" is usually the next question that people ask. Our clothing is very simple and modest. Women wear karosses made out of the whole hide of an antelope which is scraped, tanned, pulled and rubbed by the men until it is like suede. At night, men, women and children wrap themselves in karosses and sleep in them, beside their fires. By day, the men wear only their breechclouts, the children perhaps only beads, but we women wear our karosses constantly.

Plants are at the centre of our lives. I must add that, except for

UNIT 3

mangetti nuts, meat is our main source of protein. Still, vegetables make up 75% of our food — there are about a hundred plants we can eat in the Nyae Nyae region. We also use grass and branches for shelter; wood that bends for bows; firm, strong wood for digging sticks; light, strong reeds for arrows; resins for glue; light, soft wood for musical instruments, bowls, spoons and ornaments — do you see what I mean? So we, like all people all over the world, depend on our environment. We take care not to kill all the animals or use all the plants in one area. We do this by moving from one area to another and giving the plants and animals time to grow again.

!Kung people remember an animal and a plant after they have seen it once. Then we can tell the difference between that plant and any other plant, even if they look nearly the same. We get our training from doing and from watching. Mothers carry their babies with them on a gathering day and the children learn all the time. When the children can walk, they play at digging, picking and carrying the food, copying what their mothers do. Little boys play with toy bows and arrows from an early age.

1.

2.

25

UNIT 3

3.

4.

UNIT 3

5.

6.

UNIT 3

7.

8.

!U's story

Part 2:

We are gentle with our children and do not want them to be involved in work when they are still young. Besides copying the activities of adults, the play of children involves many other things like climbing trees, swinging on swings, copying the way animals carry and throw their heads and dragging babies on karosses — a favourite game. The girls and women play many different kinds of ball games. And there are many different dances that the girls do together.

Dancing and singing are very much part of !Kung life. People sing to their babies to soothe or entertain them. Everybody sings and almost everybody plays a musical instrument. Men play music on their hunting bows. The most common instrument we play is the //gwashi. It is made out of wood. Four or five thick sticks are cut into pieces of 30 centimetres in length and attached to a wooden base. Then strings are attached in slots and wound around the sticks. Playing music lightens all aspects of our lives.

Men and boys from the age of about eight to early old age play together. They play games like tug-of-war, stick throwing and these days, a game called airplane. Sometimes a boy will catch a bird, tie a cord to one leg and play airplane until the bird is too tired to flutter anymore. Then it will be left to die. To kill animals is a way of life among hunters.

And our old old people, they have a special place because the Creator has instructed the old people in the ways of life, given them knowledge of plants and digging, of arrows and poison, taught them the skills and crafts and the customs they should follow. The old old people passed on this knowledge to the generation that came after them, and so it has been passed on from generation to generation until today. We say that the young know nothing; they have no sense till they are taught by the old.

Now to get back to food. Like all people, we spend a lot of time talking and thinking about food. And providing food for the whole family takes a lot of hard work. Gathering plants is what women are made for; men are made to bring meat. But, men are not excluded from gathering whereas women are totally excluded from hunting. Women may not even touch bows and arrows.

Every able, adult woman is responsible for gathering for herself, her family and her dependants. For a woman to be lazy would be unacceptable in our society. What we do is we form gathering parties and go out and gather together. The equipment we use consists of a digging stick and containers to carry the food we have gathered. The men make the digging sticks for themselves and their wives. A root about an armslength-deep may take about fifteen or twenty minutes of digging. Then we have to carry what we have gathered in the pouches of our karosses. But the main weight we have to carry is the weight of our children. Our children are fed on breast milk until they are about four and we take them with us wherever we go — whether it's moving from one area to another to gather or to visit relatives and friends.

All !Kung men hunt. The men talk endlessly about hunting as they sit repairing their equipment and poisoning their arrows. Little boys practise shooting throughout their childhood. They hear about searching for spoor fresh enough to be worth following, about the need to act quickly once an animal has been seen, about laying down their hunting bags, quivers and spears and only carrying their bows and arrows with them when they are tracking — and about the importance of approaching silently.

At the age of about thirteen, boys begin to hunt with their fathers. This is when they practise the skills of tracking, stalking and participating in actual hunts. A young man may not marry until he has killed a big game animal — like a wildebeest, a gemsbok, a kudu or even an eland — and proved himself a hunter.

The animals and insects of Nyae Nyae supply us with many things. We use their skins for all our garments and for bags; we use their bones and horns to make tools and other things; we use cocoons to make rattles and ostrich eggshells are used for carrying water. In all these ways, nature is once again our provider.

And, when we have been without meat for some time, we love to eat it. The animals belong to no one until they are shot. A dead animal belongs to the person who kills it but the meat of the animal is shared with everyone according to custom. No one wants to seem "far-hearted" or stingy in meat sharing. The custom of sharing is something that we believe in very strongly. The person with whom one shares will share in return. The idea of eating alone and not sharing is shocking to us. Lions could do that, we say, not people.

So, every family gets a portion of the animal. Usually we cut our piece into strips and hang these strips on branches to dry. This way the meat keeps for some time.

You know, there is one thing that has always interested me. Although the women bring in most of the food that keeps the people alive, the roots and berries are often tasteless and harsh. People crave the taste of meat. And there is no splendid excitement in returning to the camp with vegetables. The return of the hunters from a successful hunt is very different. The craving for meat, the uncertainty of the hunt, the excitement of the kill and, finally, the eating and satisfaction arouse powerful emotions in people.

The words of this song express the way people feel about meat:

You must sing well.
We are happy now.
Our hearts are shining.
I shall put on my rattles,
And put on my headband,
And put a feather in my hair
To explain to God how happy we are
that he has helped us and that we
have eaten.
My heart is awake.
When we do not have meat
My heart is sad from hunger,
Like an old man, sick and slow.
When we have meat my heart is lively.

9.

10.

UNIT 3

11.

12.

UNIT 3

13.

14.

15.

!U's story

Part 3:

How big is a family and who belongs to it? A family consists of a mother, father and children. A man can have more than one wife if he wants to. Three or four families — that is between fifteen and forty people — usually live together in what we call a band. Everybody belongs somewhere and no one has no relative whatsoever with whom to live. The territory to which a person belongs may be that of his father's people or that of his mother's people: whatever territory his family is settled in will be his n!ore — that is the place in which he lives or comes from, the place to which he belongs.

We have no chiefs or political leaders. No one gets treated in a special way because of their status. People do not want to stand out or be above others because this draws unfavourable attention to them and may arouse envy and jealousy.

But, I was about to tell you about !Kung weddings. At the time of a wedding — the first marriage is usually arranged by the parents — the boy must bring an animal that he himself has killed to his bride's parents. Then the mother of the bride rubs her daughter with the fat of this animal and draws lines on her cheeks with red powder mixed with fat. All men go to live with the parents of their brides and serve them. We call this bride service. This takes the form of hunting. We explain bride service in terms of meat. The bride's family wants meat and they also want the boy to feed his bride while she is young, believing that this unites the two. Bride service should go on for long enough for three children to be born.

And, of course, there are often

fights. But, we have a way of handling conflict. We talk. When a quarrel breaks out between a husband and a wife, relatives and friends get involved and help them to stop the quarrel. We don't quarrel very often but I do remember one terrible fight I had with my husband. He tried to force me to leave with him when I wanted to stay visiting my parents. You know how he did this? He snatched my baby from my arms and walked off with him. I was so cross, I could have killed him. I ran after him and hit him on his head with my digging stick, went round in a circle stamping my feet in great, high stamps and then followed him home.

But, mostly we solve conflict by talking. To have a fight is to have failed to find a solution by other means. Fighting is dangerous — someone might get killed.

17. We !Kung, like all other people in human history, live in an uncertain world. We must face illness, bad luck and the biggest loss of all — death. Our beliefs help us to understand and accept these things. We believe in a high God, a lower god and many other spirits that bring good luck and bad luck. But the main spirits that affect our lives are those of people who have recently died — the //gangwasi. When serious illness strikes, it is almost always the //gangwasi who cause it. Longing for the living is what drives the dead to make people sick. They miss their people on earth. And so, they come back to us and put sickness into people saying, "Come, come here to me."

We have many spells, herbs and forms of magic which make people better. But, if these fail, we have the most powerful spiritual medicine or energy given by God to men and women called n/um. Trained healers have this energy.

18. To reach this energy within themselves, they usually dance all night. The women sit in a circle around the fire, clap to a rhythm and sing special medicine songs. The dancing, the singing and the clapping cause the n/um to "boil", as we say, and to rise up the healer's spines. When it "explodes" in their heads, they enter into a trance. Then they can heal the sick, change the weather and so on. Often men and women work in teams on seriously ill people.

19. And you know what I've noticed? Different people were created by God with different things to use, different skins and different medicines. The Tswana have their sangomas and their muti, the Europeans have their medicine in pills and steel needles, and we !Kung have our medicine in the form of n/um. Different medicine, very different ways of living, but when you cut any one of us, our blood flows the same colour.

16.

UNIT 3

17.

18.

19.

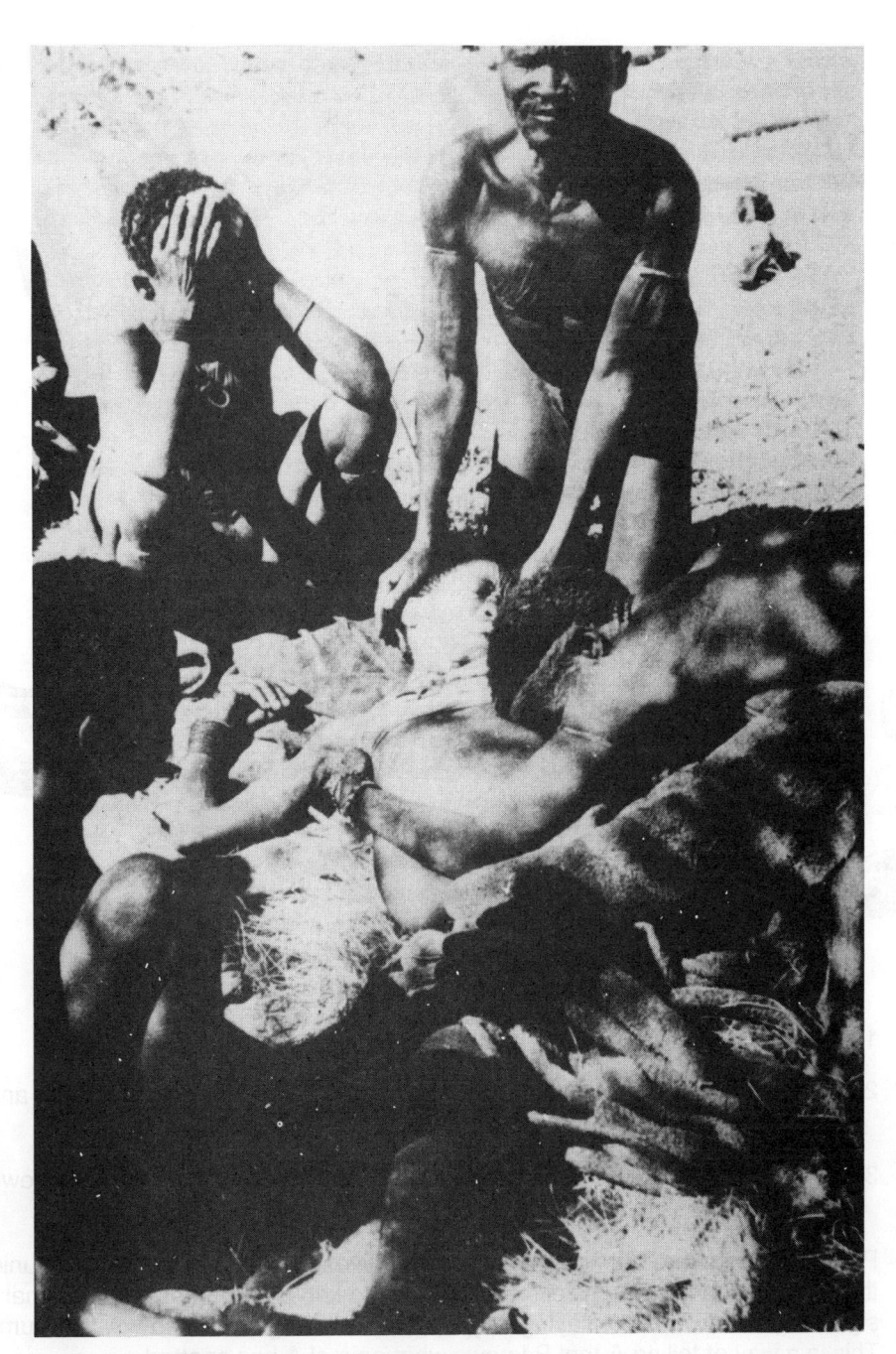

Actions speak louder than words

Hunting effectively means learning the art of approaching an animal silently. At all costs, the hunter must avoid causing the animal to take fright and escape. For this reason, hunters use hand signals to let each other know, without making a sound, what animal they have sighted.

UNIT 3

Exercise 2

Here are some of the hand signals that are used.

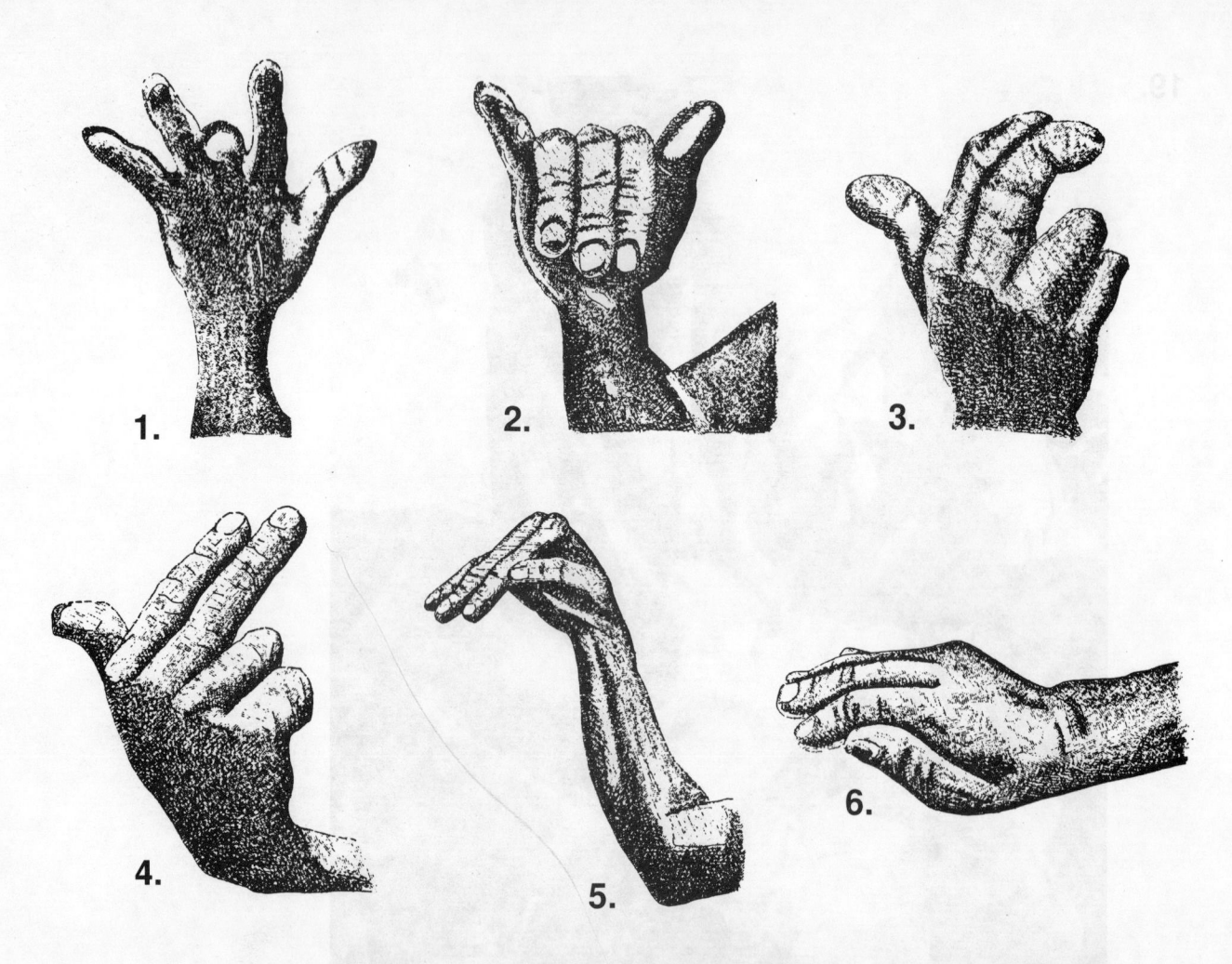

1.

2.

3.

4.

5.

6.

1. Guess what animal each hand signal represents.

2. Your teacher will write the number of each signal and the name of each animal on the board. Spend two minutes learning what each signal stands for.

3. Get into pairs. One person in each pair is A and the other person is B. Now test each other. Only A can look in the book. B close your book.

Pretend that you are out hunting together. A gives B a hand signal to communicate the animal A has seen. B looks at the board to find the number of the animal A is signalling. Then, without saying anything, B uses fingers to show A this number. This is a way of telling A that B knows what animal A has spotted.

Remember that any noise you make will frighten the animal off!

A day in the life of a hunter-gatherer

For today, you are all members of a !Kung band in Nyae Nyae. Decide whether you want to be part of a gathering or hunting party. Then do the following creative writing exercise.

38

UNIT 3

Exercise 3

THE GATHERERS . . .

You are an able, adult !Kung woman, responsible for gathering for yourself and your family. You are about to go out in your groups or gathering parties and gather for the day. Are you in the mood for gathering?

What equipment will you take with you, what plants are you likely to find and how will you carry your load, including your children?

You are likely to spend some time together gathering, observing things happening in nature, talking or singing. What kind of relationships do you have with the other members of the party? How do you feel about the day's activities?

Write a description of your day. Make it about a page long.

OR

THE HUNTERS ....

You are a !Kung man. As you know, hunting is exclusively your work. How will you prepare to go on the hunt? Is there anybody that you particularly feel like hunting with? What will you take with you? What kind of animals are you hoping to catch and what method will you use to catch them? Remember what you know about tracking, stalking and shooting.

Now go out searching for an animal. Decide what to do if/when you catch sight of an animal. How do you feel at this point? Will your party manage to shoot and kill an animal? Who will own the meat? How will you distribute it? Or will you return empty-handed with reports of the animal having taken fright and escaped?

Write a description of your day in the form of an essay. Make it about a page long.

BEFORE YOU START WRITING YOUR ESSAY

1. Think about what you want to include in your description. Make a rough outline of the main events that will take place in your story. List only about three or four events.

2. Try to think of an unusual way of starting your description. Make this your introductory paragraph. Keep it short.

3. Now use each of the events you included in your outline as the main idea of the paragraph. Develop each event by describing what "happened" in some detail. Remember to leave a line free between each paragraph.

4. Conclude your description in a memorable way. This will be your concluding paragraph.

You may feel that you want to rewrite your whole description neatly. That's a good sign! Think of what you have in front of you as a rough draft and try to improve it as you rewrite it.

UNIT 3

Tales at the fireside

You are all sitting around the fire in the camp after a hard day's hunting and gathering. Do the following exercises.

Exercise 4

Share your experiences of the day with one another. Tell each other what you wrote about in the previous exercise.

Exercise 5

The !Kung take great delight in hearing and telling stories. Listen to this tale that is passed on from one generation to the next. It has an important message for all of us. Then discuss the questions that follow.

This is the story of Kara/tuma as the !Kung tell it. It deals with a world divided into hunter-gatherers and herder-farmers.

We who were made first, have come to be last. And those who were created last, have come to be first. Even though they arrived later than we did, Europeans and Africans have come to be ahead of us.

I refuse this thing, that we should have come to be the last of all. I fear this thing. It gives me pain. And I despise that old man of long ago who caused it to happen. I think that if I saw him today I would beat him. But he's dead and there's just nothing that can be done.

That old man who was responsible for all this was named /'Tuma/'tuma. He was also called Karā/'tuma. One day long ago Karā/'tuma was out hunting. And in the bush he discovered a cow. When he saw the cow, he said, "Is this a cow? Is this a buffalo?"

And the cow was not afraid of him; it did not run away. It just stood there. But Karā/'tuma did not take it home with him to the village. Instead, he shot it. It just stood there, and he shot it. He never asked himself what is this creature that doesn't fear me, but merely shot it with his bow and arrow.

Then he went to tell the others. All the people gathered at the carcass of the cow to eat it.

Later Karā/'tuma told the African people about the cow. (The African men were his younger brothers. For Karā/'tuma's parents first bore him, then bore an African man, and last of all gave birth to a European. All of you Europeans here are small children compared to us.) He told an African man about the cows, and the African man said, "Let's go have a look at these things." So they went to see the cows. As soon as the African man saw that the cows didn't run away like other animals he said "Ai! a thing like this which doesn't fear you, you certainly don't want to kill. Let's make a kraal, and drive them into it, and see what will happen."

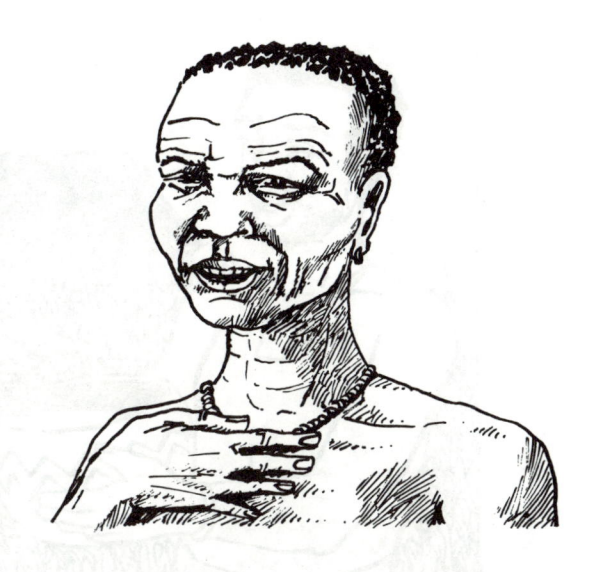

So they chopped down thorn trees and made a kraal and drove the cows into it. One of the cows gave birth in the kraal. So the African man took a thong and tied her hind legs, and she still just stood there. And he milked her, and brought the milk to Karā/'tuma.

"You've helped me find this cow, and now let's drink the milk together." But Karā/'tuma said, "Uh-uh, you eat first, and let me lick the pot!" That's what he said! "You eat first, and let me lick the pot!"

When I think about it, I want to kill him! It's a good thing he's already dead, because otherwise I'd be in jail for sure. If I had been there that day long ago, I would have killed him.

Well, the African man said, "Come on, let's eat! Lick the pot — what kind of talk is that?" But Karā/'tuma persisted, saying,

UNIT 3

"No, you eat your fill first, and let me scrape what's left off the sides of the pot."

So the African man ate, and Karā/'tuma licked the pot. When they were finished, Karā/'tuma picked up a leather thong. But the African man came and grabbed the other end of it, and they tugged at the thong to see who could pull it out of the other's hands. Finally, the African man got the thong away from Karā/'tuma. He gave Karā/'tuma a piece of string instead, saying, "You can use string to do whatever you have to do; I need the thong for my cows. You have nothing you need to tie up with leather thongs."

Karā/'tuma didn't refuse, but just took the string. Right there he should have put his foot down and fought the African man for the thong. But he didn't. He just took the string and started going about snaring animals with it. And the African man sat in comfort and milked his cows and drank the milk.

One day Karā/'tuma came across a cultivated field, a field of sorghum. He tried some, and the husks burnt his skin, made him itch. So he went into the field and started a fire, and burned most of the field, leaving a few stalks standing. Then he went back to tell the African man what he had done. "I found some terrible things over there that burn your skin. So I set fire to them. But there are some left." And the African man said, "Let's go see." And when they got to the field, he said, "Are you crazy? This is sorghum; it's food, you fool. I'm going to take what's left home with me."

Thus Karā/'tuma ruined us: that day he spoiled the chances of our people for all time.

This is how those who were made first, came to be last.

From ***Aspects of !Kung Folklore*** *by Megan Biesele, pp 322–323.*

UNIT 3

1. What is this story about?
2. What, according to this story, makes people "first"?
3. Mention two things that could cause conflict between the hunter-gatherer in the story and the herder-farmer.
4. What do these differences represent?
5. What lessons can we learn from this story?

Summing up

Sum up some of the new ideas you have learnt about in this unit by doing this last exercise.

Exercise 6

Write down five things about the San you didn't know before.

Nothing stays the same forever. Change came to the lives of many San people living in South Africa when herders arrived from further north. In the next unit, you will learn more about these herders who called themselves the Khoikhoi.

UNIT 4

The arrival of the Khoikhoi

UNIT 4

The arrival of the Khoikhoi

About 2 000 years ago (100 BC), life began to change significantly in the western part of southern Africa. Herders, also known as the Khoikhoi, arrived, bringing with them a different way of life and new ideas about the world. For the San hunter-gatherers many aspects of the Khoikhoi way of life were strange and difficult to understand.

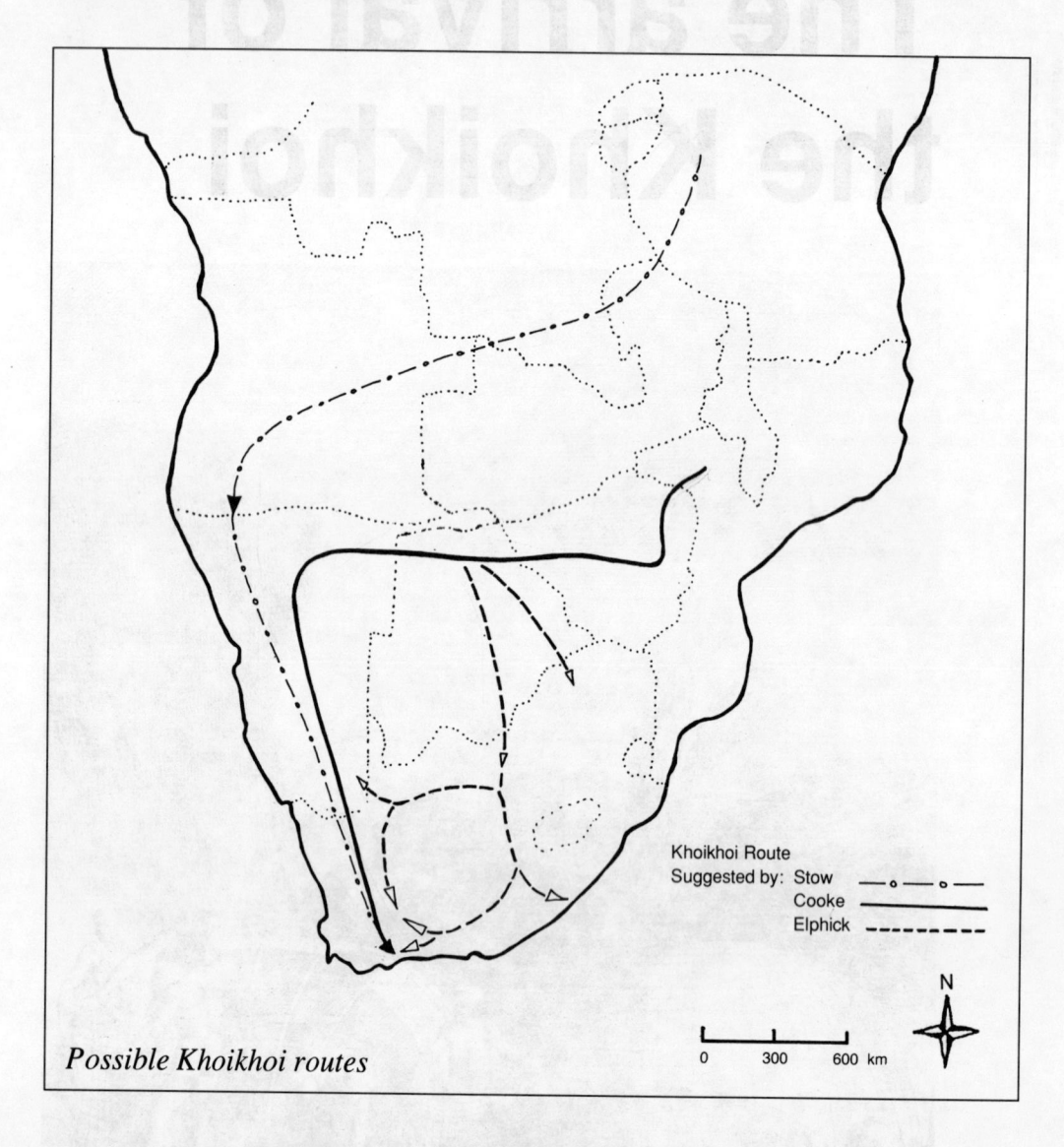

Possible Khoikhoi routes

Khoikhoi Route
Suggested by: Stow —o—o—
Cooke ———
Elphick - - - - -

0 300 600 km

This map shows the three possible routes the Khoikhoi took to southern Africa. The part of the route that Stow and Cooke agree on is based on radiocarbon dates for sites along the way. Elphick argues that his is the more likely route as there is a greater supply of water and pastures along it. He also uses evidence of similarities in the language of the descendants of people along his route and the language of the first Khoikhoi people that the European settlers met. As yet, there is no archaeological evidence to support his route. There is, therefore, still uncertainty about the exact route the Khoikhoi followed.

Who were the Khoikhoi?

UNIT 4

How can we find out who the Khoikhoi were, what their lifestyle was like and why their arrival brought about great changes?

Exercise 1

1. What do you already know about the Khoikhoi? Where did you get this information from? What name did you use for the Khoikhoi in primary school?

2. Now read this extract from a book on the Khoikhoi.

> For a long time the Khoikhoi were called "Hottentots". If we could meet the people who were called "Hottentots", they would tell us that this was not their name. They called themselves Khoikhoi which means "men of men" or "the real people". Groups used names like this to show their pride in themselves.
>
> Early European visitors to southern Africa did not know what the people who lived near the coast called themselves. The language they spoke was full of sounds which Europeans found difficult to pronounce. One of the words that the Khoikhoi used when they danced sounded like "hottentot". As a result, the Europeans began to call the Khoikhoi "Hottentots".
>
> Today, however, the word "Hottentot" has become an insult. Khoikhoi, the people's name for themselves, is used instead.

Adapted from **Men of Men** *by Candy Malherbe, pp 4–5.*

How was Candy Malherbe able to offer this explanation of how the Khoikhoi came to be called "Hottentots"? What evidence did she use?

In her book, she points out one of the **sources of information** she based her ideas on. She quotes these two extracts from the source she used, a book called **Before van Riebeeck** by R. Raven-Hart:

> "They speak from the throat and seem to sob and sigh when speaking. Their usual greeting on meeting us is to dance a song, of which the beginning, the middle and the end is 'hautitou'."

Augustin de Beaulieu wrote this in 1620. His fleet sailed from Honfleur in France to the Cape in 1619.

> "Their dance was after this fashion: on uttering the word 'Hottentot!' they snapped two of their fingers and clicked with tongue and feet, all in time ..."

Jon Olafsson, a visitor from Holland to the Cape, wrote this in 1623.

All writers of history base their information on **sources** that are available to them. There are many different kinds of **sources of information** about events in the past that writers of history can choose from.

UNIT 4

Sources of information about events in the past

Sources of information about events in the past can take many different forms.

1. Primary sources

   These are **first-hand clues** or **sources from the actual time.** Some examples of sources of information from the time include:
   - skulls, bones and artifacts such as tools, weapons, buildings or coins
   - accounts of events written at the time when they happened, photographs and paintings.

   Remember that evidence from the past is never complete. Much has happened for which all sources of evidence have been forgotten, lost or destroyed.

2. Secondary sources

   Sources about the past can take the form of **people speaking or writing about events long after they have happened.** These are called secondary sources. Information presented in secondary sources is based on evidence from primary sources.

   In an earlier unit, we saw the importance of story-telling or the oral tradition as a way of recording events in the past. This is a secondary source of information about the past. Can you explain why?

   Then, of course, there is the work of people who write history books. These writers provide us with important secondary sources of information about events in the past.

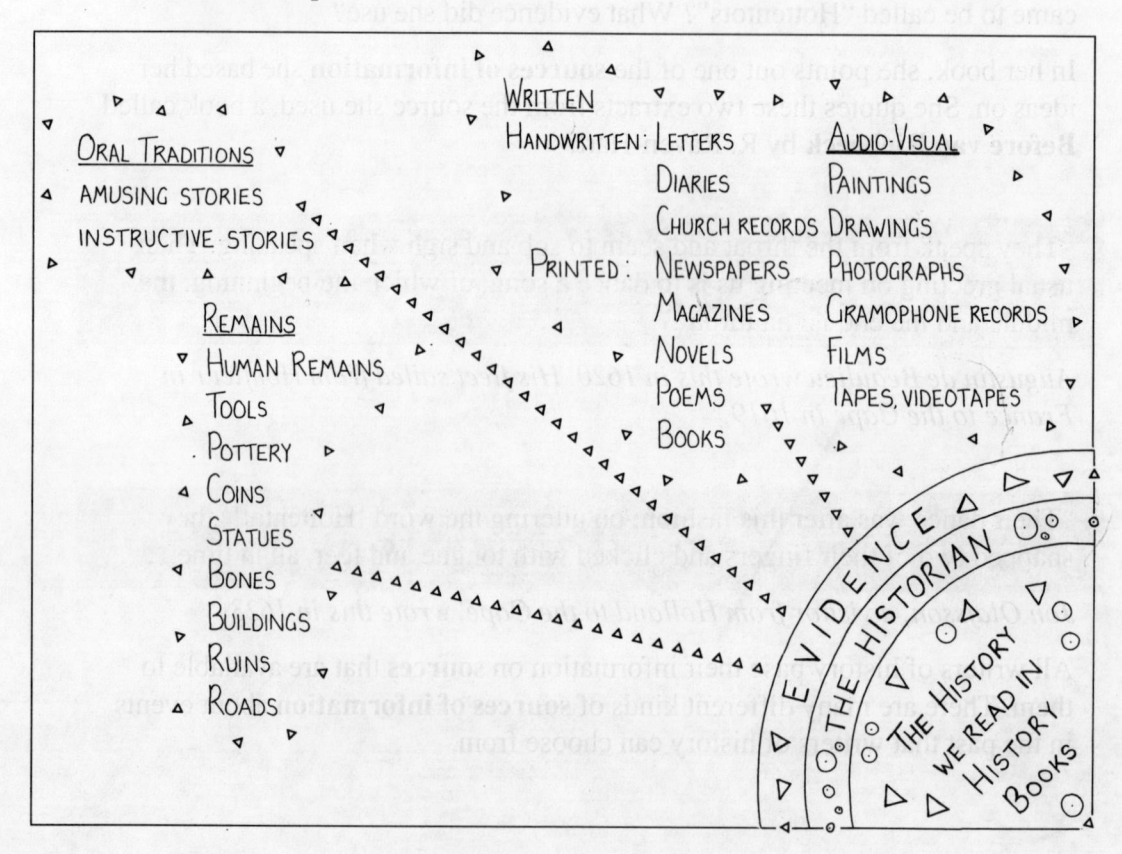

ORAL TRADITIONS
- AMUSING STORIES
- INSTRUCTIVE STORIES

REMAINS
- HUMAN REMAINS
- TOOLS
- POTTERY
- COINS
- STATUES
- BONES
- BUILDINGS
- RUINS
- ROADS

WRITTEN
HANDWRITTEN: LETTERS
DIARIES
CHURCH RECORDS
PRINTED: NEWSPAPERS
MAGAZINES
NOVELS
POEMS
BOOKS

AUDIO-VISUAL
PAINTINGS
DRAWINGS
PHOTOGRAPHS
GRAMOPHONE RECORDS
FILMS
TAPES, VIDEOTAPES

EVIDENCE → THE HISTORIAN → THE HISTORY WE READ IN HISTORY BOOKS

48

UNIT 4

Exercise 2

Discuss these questions as a class.

1. What sources of information about events in the past have already been used in this book?
2. What problems are there with using these sources to find out about the past?

Putting the picture together

Below are a number of sources which tell us about the Khoikhoi, the herders of southern Africa.

Besides the material remains, rock paintings and stories that would have been passed down, there were no other records of the way of life of the Khoikhoi — not until the arrival of the Portuguese explorers in 1488. Written information and pictures from then onwards have added to the evidence available to us of how the Khoikhoi lived.

Exercise 3

Examine these sources to find out more about the Khoikhoi. Take your time to read the extracts carefully and to look at details in the pictures. Then answer the questions that follow. To do this, you will need to refer to each source for a second time.

SOURCE 1

About 2 000 years ago the first domesticated animals — fat-tailed sheep, and a little later, cattle — and the first pottery were introduced into South Africa.

The earliest evidence is from caves in the Cape Province, like Boomplaas (near Cango). We know that the sheep must have been brought in from further north.

From **History Alive — Std 5** by J. Nisbet et al, p 113.

SOURCE 1A

UNIT 4

SOURCE 1B

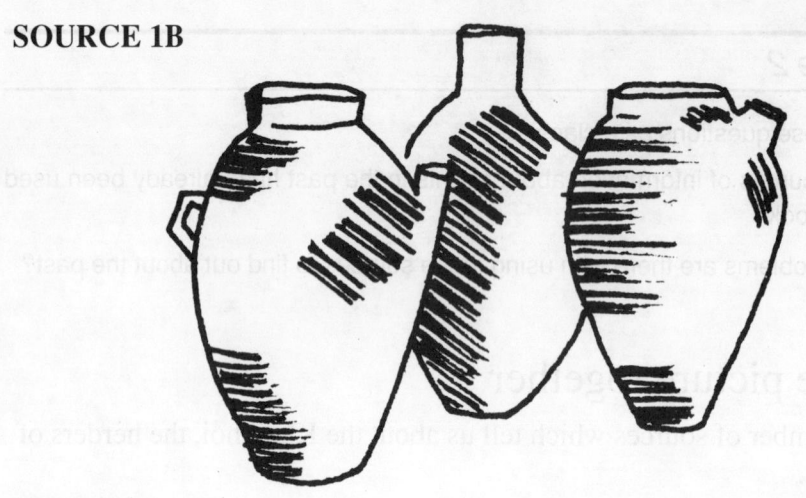

SOURCE 2

People who live as herders have to be nomads — they must move from place to place to find enough grazing for their animals. Each group of herders followed its own seasonal pattern of movement from one pasture to another. Most of them lived in the drier western half of southern Africa and seldom stayed in one place for more than a few weeks at a time.

Their possessions were limited to the amount that could be carried by themselves and their cattle. Their huts were lightly built of bent poles covered with reed mats. They could be put up or taken down in a few minutes. Even their pots and wooden milk pails were specially made with two small handles so that they could be tied onto the backs of the cattle.

From **History Alive** Std 5 by J.Nisbet et al, p 114.

SOURCE 3

"Hottentot village" from **Narratives and Adventures** by C. Williams.

50

UNIT 4

SOURCE 4

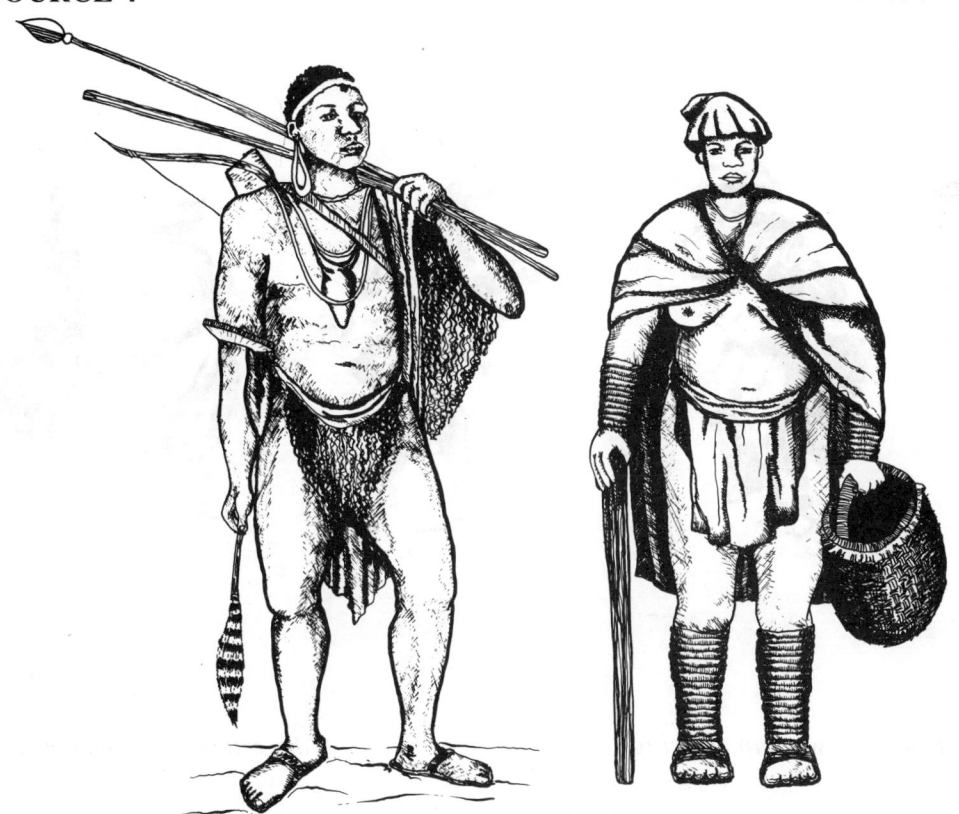

Illustrations by Heather Davidson.

SOURCE 5

. . . cattle are a sign of wealth. The Khoikhoi ate cattle that had died, or that they had captured from their enemies. They killed their animals for meat only on special occasions, like weddings and funerals.

When possible, the men killed wild animals for meat . . . Women milked the cows and ewes, and collected (gathered) veldkos, *that is, the plant foods which grow naturally. Although they were herders, the Khoikhoi also got food by hunting and gathering.*

From **Men of Men** *by Candy Malherbe, p 7.*

SOURCE 6

They continue to stamp their feet, all going round in the same circle until their dance is finished. The women stand at a distance of about ten paces, prancing and singing 'ho, ho, ho, ha, ha, ha', and clapping their hands, and from time to time they run to the men, as though enticing them. Then the men seem to want to grab them. One of these women, while running through the circle, fell head over heels in such a way that we all had to laugh, and she walked away embarrassed. She was one of the prettiest Hottentot women I had ever seen.

From **Travels of Colonel Robert Gordon** *Vol I, p 287.*

(Gordon visited the Cape in the late 1770s.)

SOURCE 7

A Khoikhoi woman dancing   17th Century artist, Anonymous

SOURCE 8

There were rich and poor people among the Khoi — unlike the San hunter-gatherers. This was because livestock did not belong to the clan* but belonged to individuals. Some people had lots, but others had few or no animals. However, rich Khoi would share their milk with poorer members of the clan.

Fat was important as a sign of wealth. They showed their wealth by smearing butter, as well as fat from their fat-tailed sheep and other animals all over their bodies. The first people to write about the Khoi did not understand these things and usually complained that the fat smelled bad to them.

Adapted from **Men of Men** by Candy Malherbe, pp 9 and 27.

SOURCE 9

30 November 1661

There are at least five different groups among these people. Early this morning the chief of one group, the Gorachoquas, came to the fort. He brought with him six head of cattle as a present, and requested that we should protect them against another group, the Cochoquas. The Cochoquas had begun to worry them in all sorts of ways. They had inspected their huts and possessions pretending to be looking for tobacco, which they knew the Gorachoquas did not possess. They had also begun to drive up their livestock so that they were grazing almost among the herds of the Gorachoquas. Moreover, they had forbidden the Gorachoquas to proceed to the Hout Bay area with their livestock because as soon as they had used up their present grazing area, they intended to occupy that area for themselves.

*Adapted from the **Jan van Riebeeck Journal** Vol 3 edited by A. A. Balkema, pp 441–2.*

New word

- clan — large family group which can increase or decrease in size depending on the reason for people coming together.

Questions on sources

SOURCE 1

1. Mention one difference between the way of life of the Khoikhoi and the San. (1)

SOURCE 2 AND 3

1. Explain how the patterns of movement of the Khoikhoi were likely to bring them into conflict with other groups. (3)

2. Why could the Khoikhoi have more possessions than the San? (1)

3. Referring to Source 2 and Source 3, describe the way their huts were constructed. (2)

4. What drink became part of the Khoikhoi diet? (1)

SOURCE 4

1. List any five items that these Khoikhoi people are wearing or holding. Then state what you think the function of each item is. (5×2 = 10)

SOURCE 5

1. Why did the Khoikhoi like to keep their sheep and cattle rather than eat them? (1)

2. What work did women do in Khoikhoi society? What work did the men do? (7)

3. In a short phrase, describe the way of life of the Khoikhoi. (1)

SOURCE 6 and 7

1. Why do you think people came together to dance in the evenings? (2)

2. Give some examples of activities that we participate in as a community today. (2)

SOURCE 8

1. How were ideas about ownership of cattle among the Khoikhoi different from the attitudes of the San to the animals they hunted? (4)

2. What reason does Candy Malherbe give to explain why the Khoikhoi smeared fat on their bodies? Can you think of another reason why this might have been a good idea? (2)

SOURCE 9

1. Describe the relationship between the Gorachoquas and the Cochoquas in 1661. (1)

2. Do you believe Jan van Riebeeck's account of the divisions between the Khoikhoi? Give a reason for your answer. (2)

UNIT 4

Identifying the kind of source

What kinds of sources of information about the Khoikhoi have we been working with?

Exercise 4

1. Draw a table containing three columns.
   a. In the first column, state the number of each source.
   b. In the second column, fill in whether each is a primary or a secondary source.
   c. In the third column, state whether it is a material remain, an oral or a written source.

2. How would an historian use these sources to tell a story about the Khoikhoi? Remember, he/she wouldn't be able to include all the information that these sources provide.

Conflict between the San and the Khoikhoi

The folktale you discussed at the end of Unit 3 highlighted some of the reasons for conflict between hunter-gatherers and herders-farmers. Can you remember what some of these reasons were?

The sources you have worked with in this unit have also shown some important differences between the Khoikhoi and the San. The next exercise will help you to understand the **effects** of the differences on the way of life of these two groups — particularly the effects on the San.

Exercise 5

This extract is the last **source** on the Khoikhoi you will work with. It examines the conflict between the San and the Khoikhoi. Read it and then check your understanding of it by answering the questions that follow.

SOURCE 10

The spread of the Khoikhoi herders into the Cape resulted in a conflict of interests with the San hunter-gatherer inhabitants of the area. A major source of conflict was competition for game — such as zebra, antelope, and wildebeest. Although the Khoikhoi were herders, they relied heavily on the
5 *spoils of the hunt for their daily food ... The Khoikhoi usually slaughtered their cattle only on special ceremonial occasions even though they provided an obvious source of protein. Also, milk from their herds was an important supplement to their diet. However, its production was often irregular and depended on the state of the pasture and the presence of new-born calves in*
10 *the herds.*

But while the Khoikhoi started competing with the San for game, their sheep and cattle were creating a further problem by denuding the pastures on which

the game was dependent. As the San watched the vast herds of game disappear, they felt justified in killing or stealing the animals that had taken the place of
15 *the game. This in turn set up a deadly cycle of raid and counter-raid, sometimes ending in full-scale warring between these groups — all of which lasted for many centuries.*

Finally, the contact and conflict between the Khoikhoi had far-reaching effects on both cultures. On the one hand, the Khoikhoi began to organise themselves
20 *into larger groups in order to form a united, stronger front against the cattle-raiding San. The San, in turn, were faced with three alternatives: some fled the continual fighting and retreated into mountain and desert areas; others established themselves into bands of robbers which raided the herds of the Khoikhoi; while others made their peace with the Khoikhoi and entered their*
25 *society as servants, hunters, herders and warriors. Many San men who chose the third option slowly obtained stock, and later, if they married Khoikhoi women, were accepted as members of these communities.*

Adapted from **Illustrated History of South Africa: The Real Story**, *p 22.*
© *1988. Reader's Digest Association South Africa (Pty) Ltd. Used with permission.*

A Khoikhoi man and his San servant

The marks given to each question give you some idea of how long your answer should be.

1. Why did the Khoikhoi need to hunt in addition to keeping herds? (1)

2. a. What is meant by "denuding the pastures" (line 12)? (1)
   b. Why did this present a problem for the San? (2)

UNIT 4

3. Why did the San feel justified in killing or stealing animals from the Khoikhoi? (1)

4. What do you think "cultures" as used in line 19 means? (2)

5. If you had been a member of a San family at the time of this conflict, which of the three alternatives presented here would you have chosen? Give reasons for your answer. (3)

Total: 10 marks

What have you found out?

The sources you have worked with in the last two exercises have given you some information about the Khoikhoi and about the sources from which history is written. Now use these sources to do the following activity.

Exercise 6

Imagine that this is an extract from the Contents page of a Std 6 history textbook.

Chapter 4: "Men of Men" — the Khoikhoi . . . .
   Herding as a way of life . . . .
   Diet . . . .
   Attitudes to possessions (including their herds) . . . .
   Dancing . . . .
   Divisions within Khoikhoi society . . . .
   Conflict between the Khoikhoi and the San . . . .

Write the chapter on the Khoikhoi that you think appeared in this history book. It needn't be more than about three or four pages long.

To do this exercise, you will have to look back to the sources on the Khoikhoi that were presented earlier in this unit. You may include illustrations if you wish.

SOME STEPS TO FOLLOW

1. Keeping your topics in mind, reread the relevant source and make notes of the information you want to include on each of the topics listed above.

2. Now develop each topic into a well-structured paragraph. Try to include the main idea in a sentence. This sentence can come at the beginning, in the middle or at the end of each paragraph.

3. If you choose to illustrate your paragraphs, trace or copy some of the illustrations from your book. You may even want to consult books or other sources for extra information and illustrations.

4. Remember to include an introductory paragraph. This could be based on the introduction to this unit.

5. Conclude your chapter on the Khoikhoi with a short paragraph that rounds things off.

> 6. Include a bibliography at the end of your chapter. This means making a list of all your sources. This is how you do a bibliography:
>
> *Yates, R: Pictures from the Past, Centaur, PMB, 1990.*
> Author — Title — Publisher — Place of Publication — Date of Publication
>
> Turn to the bibliography of **this** book to find the information you need on each source in order to compile your own bibliography.

Something to think about

The process of using sources in this way to produce a section for a history textbook is similar to what writers of history books follow. Only, they have to find their sources themselves instead of having them provided! But, like you, writers choose what to include and what to leave out. This means that every person writing about the past tells a slightly different story.

Ways of using the land

Understanding the ideas that different groups living in South Africa had about land will help you to understand one of the main causes of conflict between all the people living in this country. The struggle over the land will be discussed in detail in the units that follow.

In the meantime, refresh your memory about the way the land was used by the San and the Khoikhoi by doing the following summary exercise. This exercise involves comparing and contrasting information.

Note: When we compare, we look for similarities between things whereas when we contrast, we look for differences.

Exercise 7

You will need to refer to information on pages 24 and 34 in Unit 3 and to SOURCES 2 and 9 of this unit to help you complete the table on the next page. Copy this table onto a sheet of paper and complete it in point form. Try to list one thing that these two groups had **in common** and one way in which their ideas about the land **differed**.

UNIT 4

WAYS OF USING THE LAND	
SAN	KHOIKHOI
1.	1.
2.	2.

> ## Summing up
> The main ideas you learned about in this unit are listed below.
> 1. Khoikhoi herders arrived in southern Africa about 2 000 years ago. They brought with them a different way of life and new ideas about the world.
> 2. The spread of Khoikhoi herders in the Cape resulted in a conflict of interests with the San hunter-gatherer inhabitants of the area.
> 3. Sources of information about events in the past can take different forms.
>   a. Primary sources — these are first-hand clues or sources from the actual time e.g. skulls, coins or photographs from the time.
>   b. Secondary sources — people speaking or writing about events long after they have happened.
> 4. Every writer of history uses sources to find out information about the past. And, every writer of history chooses what to include and what to leave out.

The next very big change experienced by both the San and the Khoikhoi was in about 250 AD: the first farmers came to southern Africa from further north. In the next unit, you will find out who these farmers were and how they lived.

UNIT 5

African farmers in southern Africa

UNIT 5

African farmers in southern Africa

For a period of time that is almost impossible to imagine, all the inhabitants of southern Africa were Stone Age hunter-gatherers. Then about 2 000 years ago (100 BC), the Khoikhoi herders came south, bringing sheep with them. The previous unit considered the important changes that took place as a result of the arrival of the Khoikhoi. As we have seen, the way of life of the Khoikhoi herders soon came into conflict with that of the San hunter-gatherers.

The wheel of change had begun to turn. And, once it had been set in motion, it was to turn even faster. In about 250 AD, African farmers came to southern Africa from further north. Archaeologists call this period of history the Iron Age and we will soon see why. Like the Khoikhoi, the Iron Age farmers also had domestic animals and pottery. These farmers brought with them four important new items:

- the Bantu languages
- the cultivation of crops
- settled village life
- metal tools.

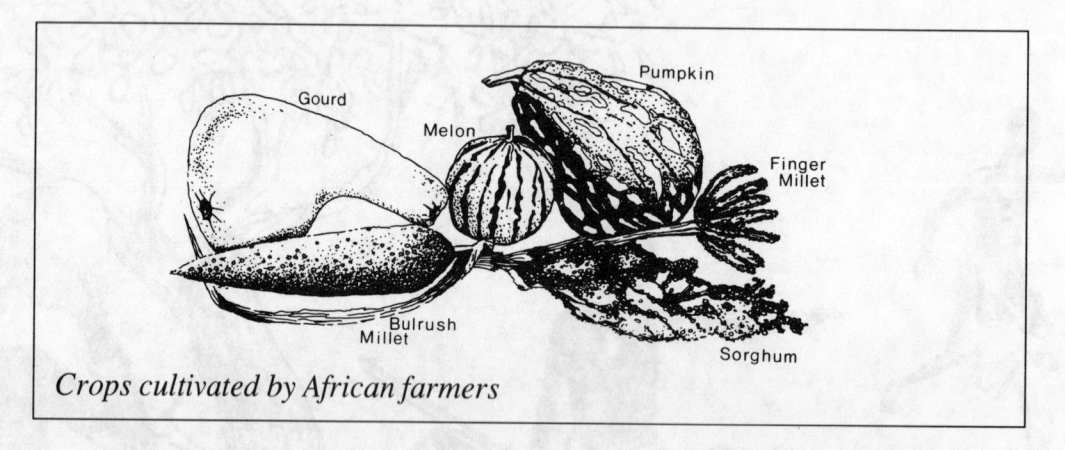

Crops cultivated by African farmers

These four aspects of life were to change the way most people lived in the eastern part of the country.

Check your mate

Before you continue with this unit, do the next exercise with your partner.

Exercise 1

Spend about ten minutes discussing these questions. Jot down your answers.

1. Can you guess why this period of history has become known as the Iron Age?
2. What do you already know about the Iron Age?
3. Choose one of the four items introduced into southern Africa. What changes do you think the item you have chosen would have brought about?

UNIT 5

The origin and settlement of African people in southern Africa

The article that follows will give you some information on the lifestyle of the newcomers. It will help you to understand how the arrival of African farmers brought a new way of life to South Africa.

> ### PREVIEWING AN ARTICLE
>
> In the following exercise, you will practise a useful reading skill. It is called **previewing**. You can probably guess what previewing means if you don't already know. Otherwise, read on and find out.
>
> Previewing means **looking for clues** to see what an article is likely to be about before you read it. To preview an article, you usually do the following:
>
> - Read the **title**. This usually helps you to guess what the article will be about.
> - Read the **blurb**. Below the title, there is often a short paragraph in bold letters. This is the **blurb**. It is designed to attract our attention and to give us more information about the contents of the article.
> - Look at the **pictures** and read the **captions**. You will remember from Unit 3 that a caption is what is written below a picture. It gives you more information about the picture.
> - Read the **subheadings** if there are any. Subheadings are headings at the beginning of every section of an article. They are like signposts which show us what information a writer has included in a passage. As you read the subheadings, make up one or two questions that you expect the article to answer.
>
> Why preview?
>
> Previewing pages gives you some idea of the information that will be presented in an article. It helps you to ask questions about what you are going to read. In this way, it makes you read with a more critical eye.
>
> Previewing also helps you to choose what you read more carefully. In a world where you have to cope with a large amount of new information every day, previewing skills are very important.

Exercise 2

Preview the article below to get some idea of what it is about. At this stage, **do not read the article.**

1. Discuss the title and blurb with a partner. What do you think this article is about? Have a second look at the pictures and captions.

2. Read each subheading again. Write down one or two questions that you expect to be answered in the information that follows each subheading.

3. Now turn to the section entitled READING TO FIND DETAILED INFORMATION on page 67.

UNIT 5

ENTER AFRICAN FARMERS

Generations of South Africans, including most of your parents, have been taught that African farmers moved south at more or less the same time as the early settlers from Europe moved north and east. The story goes that these two groups met where the Ciskei is today. However, more recent research has turned all of this on its head.

Recent research shows that Iron Age societies existed throughout the eastern part of the country centuries before the arrival of the settlers. They chose this area because it is a summer rainfall area which is suitable for growing crops. These farmers who brought the Iron Age to this part of Africa were Africans who spoke Bantu languages.

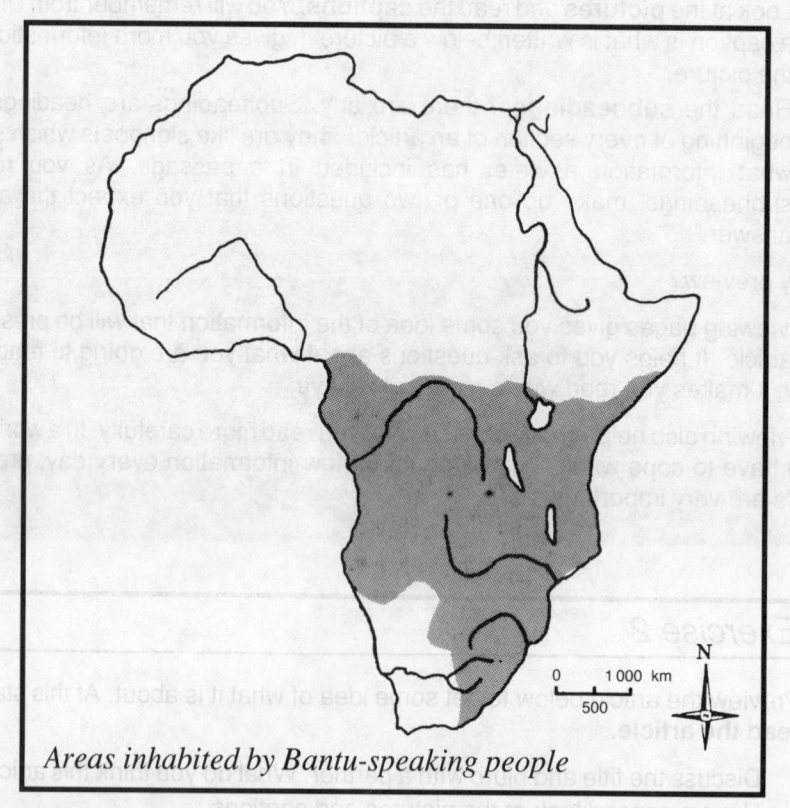

Areas inhabited by Bantu-speaking people

The cultivation of crops

With the arrival of the African farmers in southern Africa came the spread of crop farming. Martin West, in his study of this period, points out that all the African peoples were subsistence farmers to begin with. This means that each family had to produce enough for its own needs by its own labour.

Although the men still hunted for extra food, the African people were mainly herders of cattle, sheep and goats, and cultivators of the soil. This was very different from the way of life of the San hunter-gatherers who did not produce food or keep cattle.

UNIT 5

The importance of cattle

As with the Khoikhoi, cattle had great importance in these societies. Looking after the cattle was the work of the men. The cattle kraal was the social centre of the village, the meeting place of men and a place that women were usually not allowed to enter!

The herds of African farmers were larger than those of the Khoikhoi. But, as with the Khoikhoi, cattle belonged to individuals. Those who owned the most cattle had the most power. Martin West explains some of the reasons why cattle were valued so highly in African farming communities. Cattle were a considerable source of food, though more for milk than for meat. They also provided many valuable by-products such as skin for clothing and hide and horn for containers. Dung was used for fuel and for plastering walls and floors. Within these societies, cattle were also the main source of wealth and the medium of exchange. Bridewealth (lobola/bogadi) was calculated in terms of cattle. They were also used to pay fines and to ensure the goodwill of ancestral spirits.

Young boys herding cattle

UNIT 5

Women's work

Even though cattle received so much attention, survival depended on the cultivation of crops which was the work of the women. Men might help with heavy tasks such as clearing ground, but even this they regarded as a favour. The wooden hoe, later replaced by one of iron, was the main tool women used to till the fields. This made their work much easier.

Using the land

In order to farm, you need land. Land belonged to the community but individuals were given the right to use it. The chief, as head of the community, gave out the land and took it back — though he usually got advice from his headmen before he did this. Everyone had the right to some land but some people had more land or better land than other people.

Larger settlements

"Farming is hard work and takes a lot of time; livestock cannot be left to roam while people are busy with their crops. These tasks require a lot of man and womanpower," argue Malherbe and Hall. "And, in areas where cultivation is practised, the land can support greater numbers of people. Therefore, farmers usually form larger groups than herders or hunter-gatherers do."

Crop production also led to a more settled village life. It became necessary to stay in one place, close to your crops, for longer periods of time. Sturdier, more permanent houses were built and people were able to keep more possessions. These included clothing, mats, tools such as hoes and baked-clay pots for cooking, storing food or carrying water.

In most cases, Iron Age villages were made up of homesteads. A homestead housed a family in a cluster of circular houses or huts built out of poles covered with thatch and sometimes mud plaster. These huts were arranged in either a semi-circle or a full circle around the cattle kraal.

Huts arranged in a circle around the cattle kraal

"And," explain Malherbe and Hall, "in farming communities, food and seed are stored. The people who control these stores may have a lot of power over other people: they can become kings and chiefs, or important headmen. Other people must serve them and be loyal and obedient if they are to share in the food supply."

Transhumance

Living a more settled lifestyle did not mean that these farming communities did not move around at all. According to Malherbe and Hall, villages moved to a new area every few years when the richness in the soil had been used up. Similarly, farmers with cattle had to move with the seasons to make sure that their livestock obtained as much fresh grazing as possible in the spring and summer months.

We call this seasonal moving "transhumance". This movement gave land which had been heavily farmed or grazed time to rest. But such movement was very different from that of hunter-gatherers, who regularly moved to new areas, digging for plants and capturing wild animals where and when they were available.

The spread of ironworking and pottery production

And now, the explanation you've been waiting for. As the name suggests, iron was by far the most commonly used metal during the Iron Age. Iron smelting spread southwards from central and east Africa. Iron tools, according to Martin Hall, were very important to the early farmers of southern Africa. This was especially true of hoes and other implements that could be used to cut down trees and bush, break up the soil, weed the fields and harvest the crop.

Pottery production was also a very important feature of Iron Age society. Pots were used for cooking and storing food. Archaeologists often find pieces of pottery when they are excavating sites. Differences in pottery styles have helped archaeologists to tell one group from another, work out migration routes and make links between different groups.

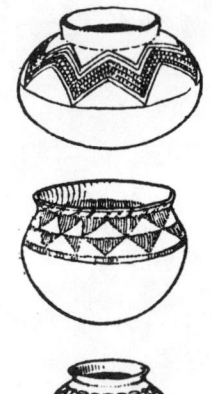

65

UNIT 5

Relationships with Stone Age groups

History Alive quotes evidence to suggest that the Iron Age people traded with and also employed some of the Stone Age people — both the San and Khoikhoi — to hunt and herd for them. In exchange for their labour and for items like beads and animal skins, the hunter-gatherers could have got food and iron implements. Some farmers intermarried with the Khoikhoi and the San. In some areas, words and click sounds from the languages of the San and the Khoi became part of the Bantu-speaking languages. Material objects of the San and the Khoikhoi are often found on Iron Age sites. This shows that, on the whole, these groups must have lived together peacefully.

According to the **Reader's Digest**, it is possible that cattle-keeping Khoikhoi made their way north to the grazing lands in the highveld and became part of the growing communities of African farmers.

However, evidence of conflict between African farmers, the Khoikhoi and the San comes from San rock paintings in the eastern Cape dating from the early 19th Century. Rock paintings like the one below show large warriors armed with spears attacking smaller figures armed with bows and arrows. They show the clash between two ways of life — hunter-gathering and settled agriculture — that occurred in some parts of the country.

As the Reader's Digest notes, "A metal plough will slice through unyielding soil, a decorative bangle will entice a mate, an arrow head will drive deep into an enemy's flesh. It follows, therefore, that people who know how to smelt and work iron must triumph over those who do not."

UNIT 5

Reading to find detailed information

The information contained in the article you have just previewed is based on 4 different sources. They are:

- Malherbe, C and Hall, M: *Changing the Land*, Shuter & Shooter, Pietermaritzburg, 1988.
- Nisbet, J et al: *History Alive Std 6*, Shuter & Shooter, Pietermaritzburg, 1985.
- *Illustrated History of South Africa: The Real Story*, Reader's Digest Association South Africa, Cape Town, 1988.
- West, M: *Abantu*, Struik, Cape Town, 1976.

Now do the following exercise.

Exercise 3

Go back to page 62 and read "Enter African Farmers" through carefully.

See whether or not the article contains the answers to all the questions you asked when you were previewing. What other questions could you have asked and found answers for?

How one thing led to another

The question we often ask about the past is, "Why did this happen?" By asking this question, we are trying to work out the **CAUSE** or number of causes that made something happen (**EFFECT**). This "something" usually becomes a new **CAUSE** that makes something else happen. That is how life works: one thing usually leads to another.

Here is a common example of how one thing can lead to another. See whether you can work out the **cause** and the **effect** of each action.

UNIT 5

Here is another example:

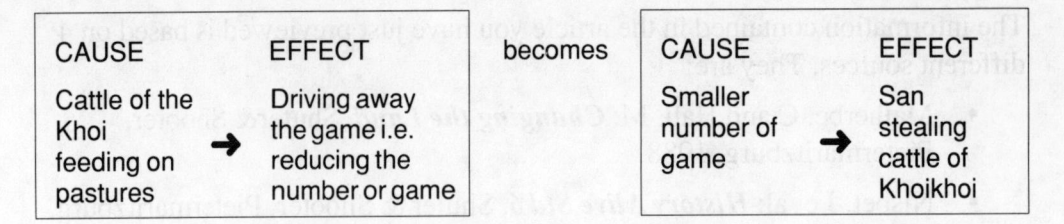

CAUSE	EFFECT
Cattle of the Khoi feeding on pastures →	Driving away the game i.e. reducing the number or game

becomes

CAUSE	EFFECT
Smaller number of game →	San stealing cattle of Khoikhoi

African farmers introduced new things into southern Africa. These new things **caused** other things to change. The next exercise looks at some **effects** of the arrival of African farmers in southern Africa.

Exercise 4

Below are a number of **CAUSES** and **EFFECTS** presented in the form of pieces of a puzzle. But, they are all mixed up. Copy the information contained in each puzzle piece onto a sheet of paper and draw a square around each one. Then see if you can work out what **cause** led to what **effect** by filling in an arrow pointing to the right box. Do this in pencil. Remember that

- a cause can have more than one effect
- an effect can have more then one cause.

You may therefore have a number of arrows coming from one cause and a number of arrows pointing to one effect.

You can expect to have as many as ten arrows going in different directions. There is no one right answer to this exercise but you should be able to explain your arrows. Remember to leave enough space for your arrows.

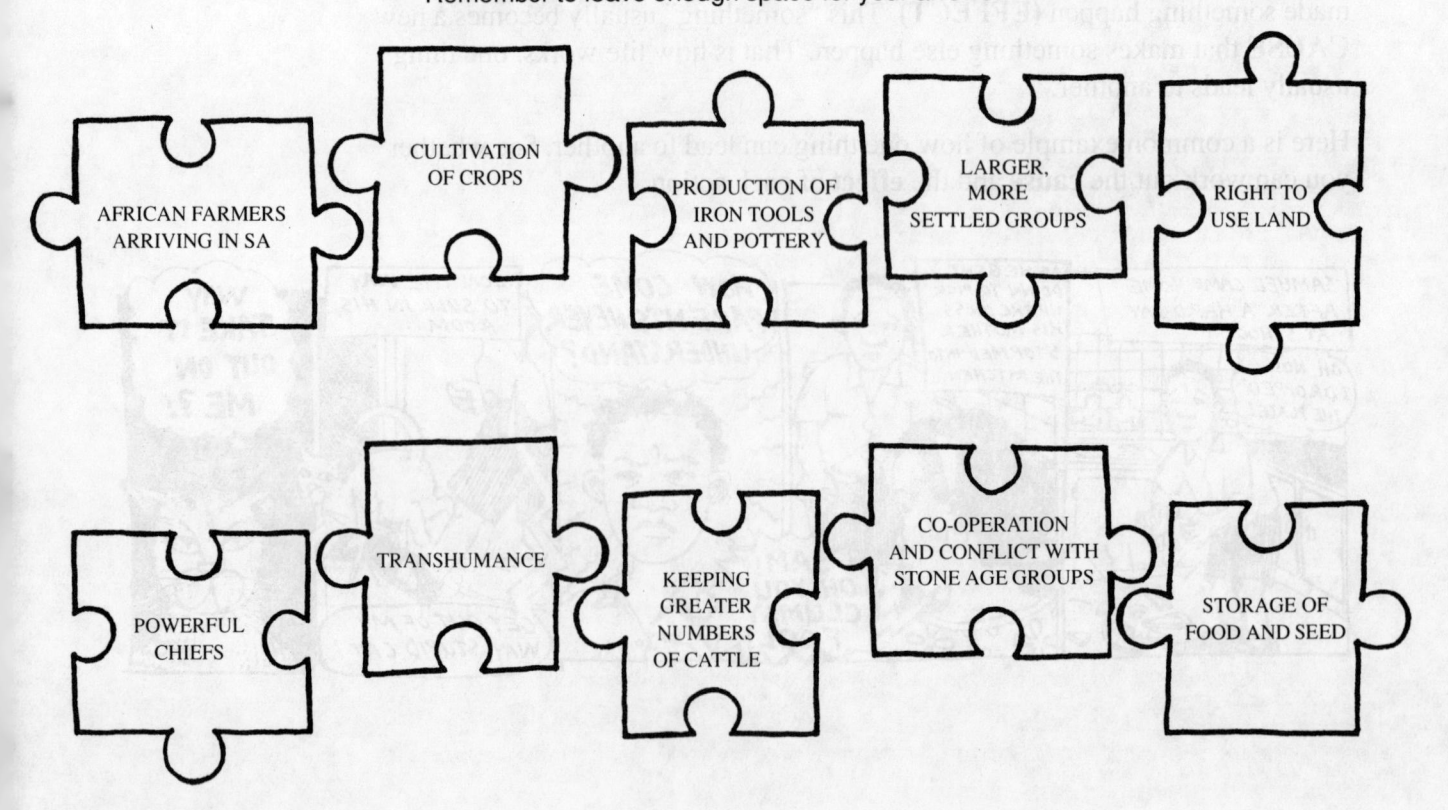

Puzzle pieces:
- AFRICAN FARMERS ARRIVING IN SA
- CULTIVATION OF CROPS
- PRODUCTION OF IRON TOOLS AND POTTERY
- LARGER, MORE SETTLED GROUPS
- RIGHT TO USE LAND
- POWERFUL CHIEFS
- TRANSHUMANCE
- KEEPING GREATER NUMBERS OF CATTLE
- CO-OPERATION AND CONFLICT WITH STONE AGE GROUPS
- STORAGE OF FOOD AND SEED

The ancestors of today's African people in southern Africa

Most of South Africa's African people are from four Bantu language groups: Nguni, Sotho, Tsonga and Venda. These groups all shared the basic elements of the Iron Age way of life.

The two largest of these language groups, the Nguni and the Sotho, are today subdivided into a number of different languages. The table that follows shows what these subdivisions are.

MAIN LANGUAGE GROUP	SUBDIVISIONS
Nguni	Zulu
	Xhosa
	Swazi
	Ndebele
Sotho	Tswana
	South Sotho
	North Sotho (Pedi)

Much historical information about these groups has come to us through the **oral history** remembered by the people themselves. A great deal of this information concerns the past of particular royal families.

Another very important source of evidence about the origins of African people in southern Africa is **archaeology**. Because it deals with material culture, it can tell us little about particular leaders or events. Instead, it gives us information about the way of life of the ordinary people in a village.

The case study that follows is based largely on archaeological evidence that has been found in the Transvaal.

The ancestors of the Tswana people: A case study using pictures

The pictures and information used in this section are based on archaeological research done in and around Johannesburg by Professor Revil Mason. As far as we know, the earliest African people in this area were the ancestors of the Tswana people. By looking at the following scenes, we can discover many things about the way of life of the ancestors of the Tswana people in 1600 AD, about 200 years before Europeans first arrived in the Transvaal.

UNIT 5

Exercise 5

1. Divide into groups of five or six. Each group will be given one of the pictures below to work with. These pictures show scenes from a Tswana village in about 1600 AD. They give you some detailed information about the Iron Age way of life that African farmers followed.

2. Your task is to set a short comprehension exercise in which you ask five questions about the picture you have in front of you. Be careful not to ask questions that can be answered by just saying "Yes" or "No"

    • One person in the group must **write the questions down neatly** on a separate sheet of paper so that another group will easily be able to read them. **Leave space** after each question for the answer to be filled in.
    • Write the number of your picture clearly at the top of your page of questions.

3. Now swop comprehension exercises with another group. In your groups, discuss the answers to the questions you have received. In some cases, you may need to invent an answer e.g. the name of a person. In a case like this, there is no right or wrong answer.

One person from the group should write the answers in pencil in the space provided after each question.

4. Your teacher will now give you some information on the picture you are discussing. After reading this information, consult with each other about what changes you want to make to your answers.

5. The next step involves getting back the questions your group set and reading the answers.

6. Each group elects a person to give a brief reportback on their picture, commenting on the questions they set and the answers they received. Look at the relevant picture in your book during each reportback. On a separate sheet of paper, make notes about each picture based on the reportbacks.

1.

UNIT 5

2.

3.

71

UNIT 5

4.

5.

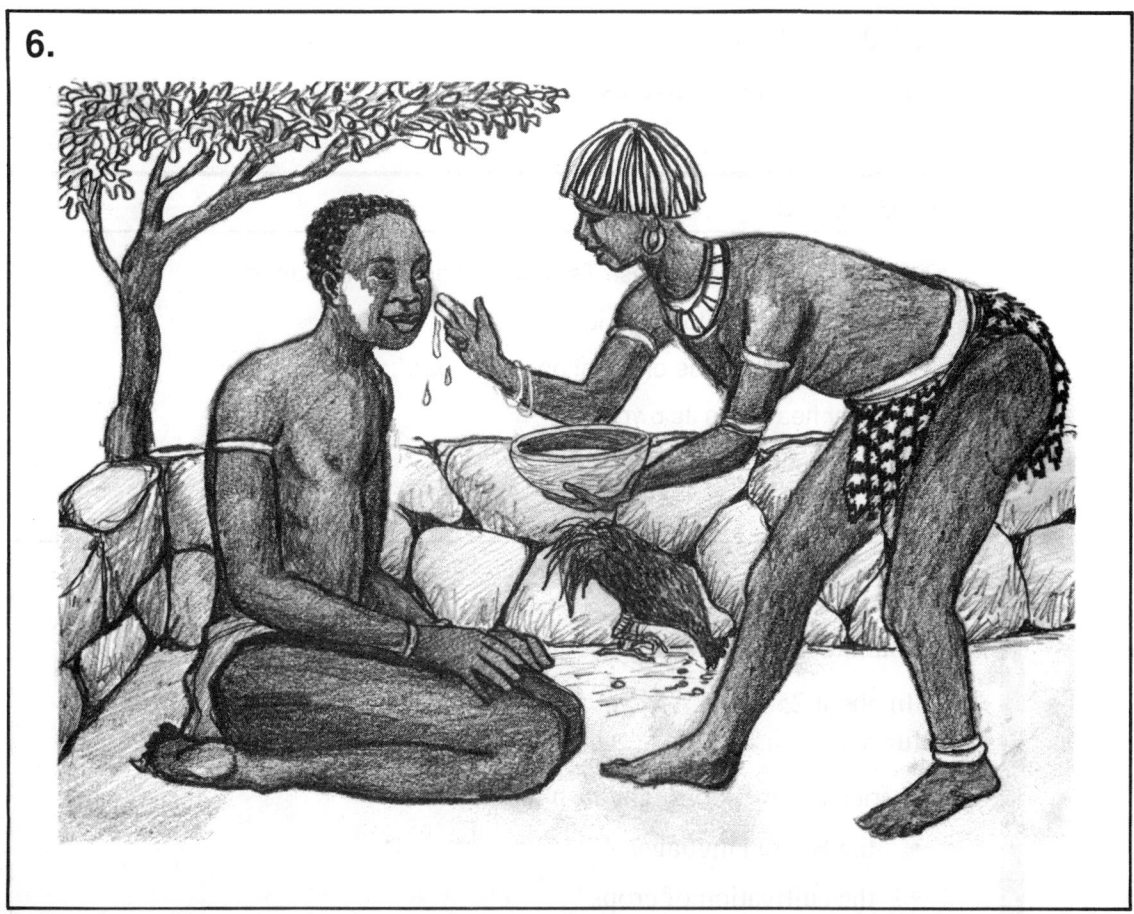

UNIT 5

6.

7.

UNIT 5

Tswana proverbs

What role do you think proverbs play in a society?

Exercise 6

Discuss the meaning of these Tswana proverbs with a partner.

"To overfill the pot is to break it."

"The lion that kills is the one that does not roar."

"The bitter heart eats its owner."

"There are many dawns."

Summing up

The main ideas you learned about in this unit are:

1. In about 250 AD, African farmers came to southern Africa from further north.

2. African farmers brought with them
   - the Bantu languages
   - the cultivation of crops
   - settled village life
   - metal tools.

3. Conflict between San hunter-gatherers and these African farmers occurred in some parts of the country. This often took the form of a fight over land.

4. The case study of the Tswana people gives us some idea of how African farmers in southern Africa lived.

Meanwhile, back in the western Cape, some dramatic events were about to take place. Several ships were sailing into Table Bay. Read on and find out how the Khoikhoi reacted when strangers arrived from beyond the sea.

UNIT 6

The struggle over land:

Khoikhoi meet Dutch

UNIT 6

The struggle over land: Khoikhoi meet Dutch

In Europe in the 1600s, the world was changing. Until then, most people had lived off the land. Now trading started to gain importance.

The Dutch East India Company based in Holland became a powerful trading company in the 17th Century. Many ships from Europe used to stop at the Cape on their way to and from the East to trade. The next group of people to settle in South Africa were the Dutch who started a refreshment station at the Cape. The first people they met were the Khoikhoi.

As the number of people in South Africa increased, there was more competition for the land. Because land is so necessary for survival, especially for herders and farmers, most people wanted the use of as much land as possible. Not surprisingly, different groups of people had different ideas about who owned the land and how it should be used. As a result, there were many conflicts over the land. These conflicts often led to bitter wars in which many people lost their lives.

Ideas about land

Land is the most important source of wealth in any society. Can you think of the reasons for this?

People need land to build their homes on. Game and herds of domestic animals, which can provide food for people, need land for grazing. Farmers need land on which to grow the crops that feed people. The minerals, like iron, copper and later, diamonds and gold, extracted from the land provide the raw material for tools, machinery, ornaments and jewellery. These minerals can also be bartered or sold in various forms.

This next exercise will help you to work out the ideas about land that many people have today.

Exercise 1

In pairs, answer the questions that follow based on this common sign:

UNIT 6

1. What does "private property" mean?
2. What is a "trespasser"?
3. Why would a hunter-gatherer have found it difficult to understand what a "trespasser" was?
4. Would a herder have believed in "private property"? Explain your answer.
5. How do you think an early farmer would have reacted to this sign?
6. Why do notices like this always have "By order" at the end? What does this mean?

Something to think about

The idea of private ownership of land has not always existed. Certainly, it had no place in hunter-gatherer society. People owned cattle in the herding communities you have learnt about but they did not **own** land.

In farming communities, everybody had the right to use the land to grow crops and graze cattle. But, nobody **owned** the land. The chief, as the head of the community, gave out the land and took it back.

So, where do you think the idea of owning land comes from? To answer this question, we need to understand that different people who came to South Africa had different ideas about land. Knowing what these different ideas were will help to explain why attitudes to land changed so much after the arrival of the settlers from Europe.

Strangers from beyond the sea

Imagine two groups of people from completely different worlds seeing each other for the first time . . .

The age of exploration had dawned for Europe. Navigators from Portugal were risking their lives on the high seas to extend the boundaries of their known world. In 1488, some Khoikhoi were seen by Bartholomew Dias at Mossel Bay when his ship stopped there en route to the East. This is how he described them:

SOURCE A

. . . we sighted land in a bay which we called the Angra dos Vadqueiros [Bay of Cows], *because of the many cows seen there, watched by their herdsmen. And since they had no language which could be understood, we could have no speech with them; but rather they drove off their cattle inland, as if terrified at such a new matter, so that we could learn no more of them than that they were blacks, with woolly hair . . .*

From ***Before van Riebeeck*** *by R. Raven-Hart, p 1.*

UNIT 6

A Khoikhoi family and their herd

Compare his description of the Khoikhoi with Krotoa's when she first saw the Dutch settlers. Krotoa was the first Khoikhoi woman to live amongst the Dutch at the Cape. She was sent as a young girl to learn Dutch in Van Riebeeck's household. This is what a modern writer imagined Krotoa observed on her arrival:

SOURCE B

Nothing she had heard about the Dutch from her uncle and the other men had prepared Krotoa for what she saw when they arrived at the place where they were to meet Commander van Riebeeck. There were a few Khoikhoi men standing around, curious to see what was going on. But most of the people waiting to greet them were of such a strange appearance that Krotoa could not tell whether they were men or women. They all had long hair curling down over their shoulders, or sticking out wildly from under caps or broad, floppy hats. Many of them also had hair growing all over their faces. It was only when they started speaking to each other in deep, gruff voices that she realised they must be men.

Although the sun was beating down on them, they all wore several layers of clothing, covering their bodies from wrist to ankle, and some even had big karosses of thick cloth hanging over their shoulders. They all wore heavy leather boots. The colours of their clothes delighted Krotoa, and she envied all the metal ornaments they wore. But how uncomfortable they must be, wrapped up in all that cloth. Indeed, although some were taller than the Khoikhoi men, they all looked very thin and unhealthy, and their skins were burnt red from the sun.

Adapted from **Krotoa** by Karen Press, pp 21–2.

UNIT 6

Krotoa meeting some of the Dutch settlers

Stepping into other people's shoes

In this next activity, you are going to be put into different situations. See how you react!

Exercise 2

Stage 1

Divide into two large groups, A and B. Now, form groups of four people within your large group. All the **A groups** do **Part A** of this exercise. The **B groups** do **Part B**.

Read and discuss all the situations that are described on the next few pages. Elect a note-taker to summarise your answers to the questions which follow each situation.

In cases where the group cannot agree on an answer, write down the different responses. You need to respond to each situation quite quickly as you only have 30 minutes to do this part of the exercise.

PART A
SITUATIONS

1. You live in a coastal settlement in an area which gets winter rain. People in your community own large numbers of sheep and cattle. You spend most of the day gathering food or tending animals. You do not grow crops as you don't have crops that would grow in the dry summer. It is mid-summer and the pastures in the area in which you have settled have been completely grazed by your animals.
   a. How do you feel?
   b. What do you do?

2. A ship sails into the bay. Strangers from another country come ashore. You cannot communicate with them because they speak a different language. They

UNIT 6

help themselves to water and gesture for some of your animals as they need fresh meat. They have knives, iron, copper ornaments, clay pipes and tobacco.
  a. How do you feel?
  b. What do you do?

3. Some of you throw stones at the strangers who are taking water. One of the strangers uses a crossbow and kills a member of your group. A fight breaks out. You use your animals, especially your oxen, to protect yourselves and to terrify your enemy. You manage to injure several of the strangers. They take revenge by attacking your settlement.
  a. How do you feel?
  b. What do you do?

4. For a while, relations are very tense every time strangers visit your shore. Many of them have guns and horses! Your skilful use of your animals helps you to hold out against the superior weapons of the strangers. Slowly the situation improves and some trading begins. The strangers need your meat and you need their iron for making spears. You also enjoy smoking their tobacco very much. However, it eventually becomes clear that the strangers are not just visiting but are creating a permanent settlement that is growing all the time.
  a. How do you feel?
  b. What do you do?

5. Some of the strangers take over areas of land and start to farm crops. This style of farming means that they settle in one place instead of moving from place to place to avoid overgrazing the way you have always done. Also, they prevent you from using the streams on "their" property — streams which anyone in the area had been free to use before.
  a. How do you feel?
  b. What do you do?

6. Although the strangers need labourers to farm their crops, they have the sense not to try to force you to work for them. They rely too much on your livestock to risk damaging their relationship with you in this way. Instead, they bring slaves from another country to work on "their" farms.
  a. How do you feel?
  b. What do you do?

7. The strangers, it seems, are here to stay! They take over more and more land. You have to fight to keep the land you are using, your water resources, your livestock and your independence. This causes bitter conflict. The strangers defend themselves by building a castle and setting up several outposts from which they keep watch. They also patrol the area on horseback and use guns against you to steal your cattle.
  a. How do you feel?
  b. What do you do?

Now that you have discussed all seven situations, decide on a short message or statement which, with the help of an interpreter, you want to communicate to the strangers. Write this message in big, bold letters on a piece of paper or newsprint.

UNIT 6

PART B

SITUATIONS

1. You are part of a crew on a long sea voyage. You have experienced months of terrible hardship. Death has stared you in the face as your ship has been tossed by the high seas. Also, you have run out of fresh water and food. You enter a bay situated at the foot of a mountain, where there are abundant fresh-water streams.
    a. How do you feel?
    b. What do you do?

2. You take on shore with you guns and crossbows for protection, knives and some iron and copper ornaments. The smokers amongst you take their pipes and some tobacco. In the distance, you see a group of herdsmen watching over fat, healthy cattle.
    a. How do you feel?
    b. What do you do?

3. Although the people you meet speak a different language, you manage to communicate a greeting. They are very suspicious of you. Because of your desperate thirst, you rush to drink from the first streams you see. Now you need to ease your hunger pains. The locals seem to be guarding their cattle very carefully. They start throwing stones at you. Members of your crew get angry. A fight breaks out in which one of the locals is killed and several of your crew get injured.
    a. How do you feel?
    b. What do you do?

4. Over time things settle down. You realise that you are in a land of plenty. There is a great deal of water and you are able to barter cattle from the locals. But, you still have to rely on crops, like rice and wheat, that come to you from other countries. It would be much better to become self-sufficient by settling permanently at the Cape and growing your own crops. Future ships passing by would benefit greatly from a supply of water, wheat and meat.
    a. How do you feel?
    b. What do you do?

5. The Company you have sailed to this land with, manages to expand into areas used by the locals. As a result, you are given a smallholding on which to farm fruit, vegetables and grain for yourselves and for passing ships.
    a. How do you feel?
    b. What do you do?

6. Farming land is very hard work and you soon realise that you are going to need extra labour. The locals are not likely to work for you because they neither need to nor want to. They have enough work tending their cattle, hunting and gathering. The Company imports slaves to work for you.
    a. How do you feel?
    b. What do you do?

7. Over time your settlement grows and starts doing very well. This leads to conflict with the locals who raid your farms, stealing your cattle and destroying your crops. You need to be able to defend yourself against them.
    a. How do you feel?
    b. What do you do?

UNIT 6

Now that you have discussed all seven situations, decide on a short message or statement, which with the help of an interpreter, you want to communicate to the locals. Write this message in big, bold letters on a piece of paper or newsprint.

Stage 2

All the groups that did Part A should gather on the one side of the classroom while the groups that did Part B should gather on the other side. Hold up the messages you want to communicate to those on the other side of the classroom. Take turns to read them out.

Discuss these messages as a class. Try to find out why the other group feels as it does. Ask them questions about past events. Refer to your notes to help you ask and answer questions. Your teacher will guide the discussion.

Some facts . . .

Although many things which are called "facts" in history are often interpretations, there is agreement about some events in the past. The following is based on the archaeological, written or oral evidence available to us about these events.

You will by now be aware that the situations you have just discussed are based on what happened from the time when the first explorers came into contact with the Khoikhoi on the shores of the south-western Cape until the Dutch settlement was firmly established. The information below is based on the evidence — mainly in the form of written documents — that is available to us about this period of our history.

Exercise 3

Read this information quietly on your own. Try to **pick out some of the main ideas** it contains. Look for ideas about the conflict between the Khoikhoi and the European settlers. You will need to use these ideas in the next exercise.

Reading for the main idea is called **skimming**. It is a useful study skill as it helps you to find and to remember the main points of what you read. Once you have skimmed this information, you will probably need to go back to the beginning and read it through again more carefully.

- Trade developed from 1591. The Dutch and English ships rounding the Cape needed supplies of water, meat and vegetables. The Khoikhoi wanted iron for tips to their spears and arrows. By 1610, a surplus of iron had developed, and copper and tobacco were then in demand.

- The Khoikhoi traded their livestock, especially between 1590 and 1615. But, the amount they traded was decided by their own needs. They controlled their prices and the number of cattle they traded in a way that gave their chiefs a great deal of power. When it suited them, the Khoikhoi withdrew from trade and avoided the Europeans.

- In 1652, a refreshment station was established under Jan van Riebeeck at the Cape by the Dutch East India Company. This station soon became a

Trading in Cape Town

permanent settlement for the Dutch. The aim of the station was to supply Company ships with meat and other food on their way to the East.

- Some settlers were given land by the Company to farm in the Cape in 1657. They were known as free burghers. There was conflict between the free burghers and the Khoikhoi. The free burghers settled on land that the Khoikhoi had previously used. They stayed in one place and used intensive farming methods to produce fruit, vegetables and grains. They got their seed from Europe.

- The style of farming of the Dutch came into conflict with the lifestyle of the Khoikhoi herders. The permanent settlements of the European farmers upset the seasonal movement of Khoikhoi communities as more and more land became unavailable to those communities. Also, in the past, anybody had been entitled to use water. Now, settlers were denying the Khoikhoi use of streams on the land the settlers had claimed for themselves.

- The Khoikhoi fought against this by using their cattle to trample the crops of the free burghers and by refusing to sell cattle to them. This tempted the settlers to start their own herds. Sometimes cattle were stolen from the Khoikhoi.

- For a long time the Khoikhoi resisted becoming labourers on the farms of the settlers. This was one of the reasons why slaves from other African and Asian countries were brought to the Cape.

- The Khoikhoi used their oxen to protect themselves from the settlers in the way that tanks are used today. They also used their animals to terrify their enemies.

UNIT 6

The Khoikhoi used their oxen to protect themselves and to terrify their enemies

- On 19 April 1672, the Khoikhoi ceded* all of the Cape of Good Hope, from Lions Head along Table Bay, including Hout and Saldanha Bays to the Dutch. In exchange for this land, a treaty stated that the Dutch would pay in the form of goods worth 10 000 guilders. In the end, the treaty was not honoured and the Khoikhoi received goods worth only 85 guilders for this land. *(Moodie, D: **The Record** pp 317 - 8)*. The Dutch agreed to other similar treaties which they did not honour.

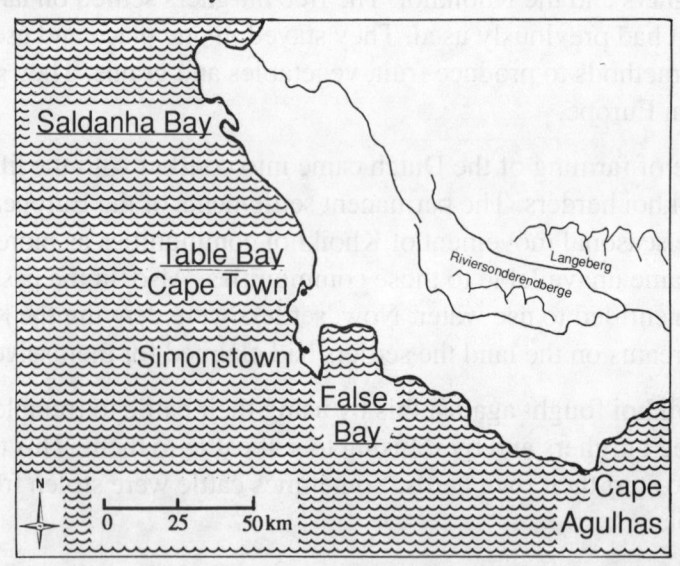

- Towards the end of the 17th Century, the Company no longer relied completely on the Khoikhoi for cattle. It had accumulated its own herds. It also no longer saw the Khoikhoi as a threat as it had worked out an effective system for defending itself: Company officials built outposts and patrolled the area on horseback; the Company provided isolated farmers with guns and built a castle so strong that it still exists today.

The Castle gate

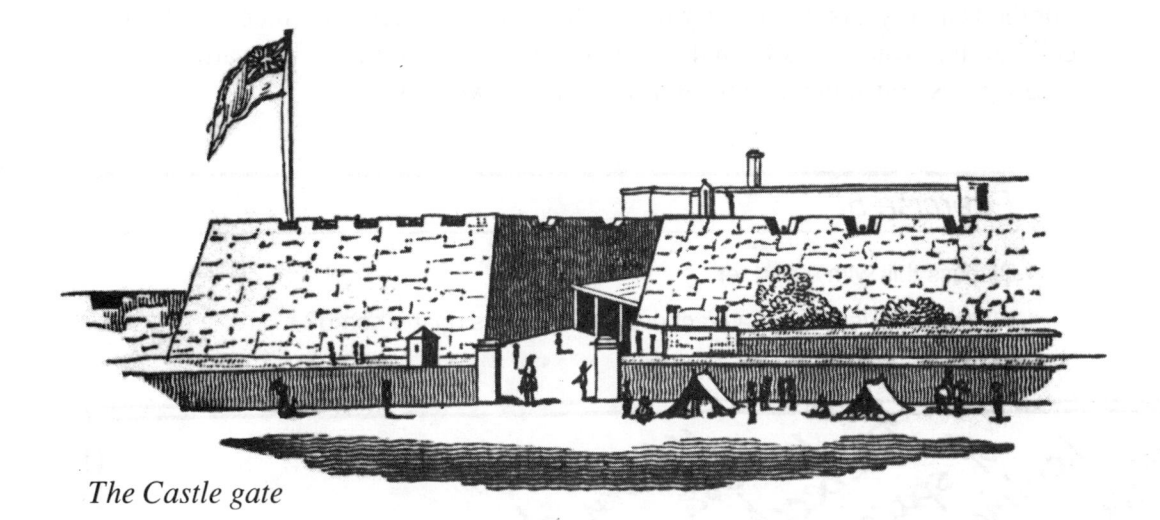

- Between 1672 and 1701, the Khoikhoi were defeated by the Dutch a number of times. Over time, they lost more and more of their land and their cattle to the settlers. The Dutch also involved themselves in raiding among the Khoikhoi. With their guns, the Dutch could help a Khoikhoi group to defeat its enemies. As the Company interfered more in the affairs of the Khoikhoi (e.g. by including the Khoikhoi in the legal system of the Company), power began to be taken away from the chiefs. By the turn of the century, many Khoikhoi were forced to become labourers on the farms of the settlers in exchange for tobacco, bread, alcohol, milk and vegetables.

- Within fifty years of the establishment of Dutch settlement in 1652, the Khoikhoi communities of the south-western Cape had lost their land, water resources, most of their livestock and their independence.

- Then came the smallpox epidemic of 1713, brought to the Cape through a parcel of infected linen from a visiting Dutch ship. More than one in ten people living in the Cape died of this disease. Many Khoikhoi died as they had less resistance to this disease than the Dutch had.

New word

- ceded — gave up their rights (especially to land)

Tying events together

You have looked at the effects on the Khoikhoi of the arrival of the Dutch settlers at the Cape from a number of different angles. Now do this exercise.

Exercise 4

With a partner, discuss the effects of the arrival of the Dutch settlers. Which of these effects do you think was the most important? Why?

UNIT 6

And now for something completely different

For the last 40 years, the history of South Africa has been presented to school children like yourselves from the point of view of the settlers. The cartoon below gives you some idea what most students were taught.

Exercise 5

Discuss this with a partner.

What would you say to a teacher who wrote this on the board?

History started in South Africa in 1652, with the arrival of Jan van Riebeeck. Until he arrived there was just a lot of space with a few Hottentots wandering about herding goats and smearing their bodies with fat. There were also scattered bands of ignorant Bushmen who stole everything they saw.

From the **Cape Times** *by Tony Grogan, 1985*

Something to think about

It is a fact worth thinking about that the oppression of the people of southern Africa by the Europeans began, not because statesmen or settlers wanted it, nor because it had to be that way; but because thousands of ordinary people, white and brown, quietly followed their goals, not realising the terrible results this would have.

Adapted from **The Khoikhoi and the Founding of white South Africa**
by Richard Elphick, p 239.

Summing up

The main ideas you learned about in this unit are listed below.

1. In 1652 a refreshment station was established under Jan van Riebeeck at the Cape by the Dutch East India Company.

2. Conflict between the Khoikhoi and the Dutch arose because the Dutch settled on land that the Khoikhoi had previously used.

3. The Khoikhoi signed several treaties with the Dutch in which they gave up their rights to some of the land. The Dutch were supposed to give the Khoikhoi goods in exchange for this land. The Dutch usually did not give the Khoikhoi what they had agreed to in the treaties.

4. By the end of the 17th Century, the Khoikhoi communities of the south-western Cape had lost their land, water resources, most of their livestock and their independence.

The next unit looks at one example of how the relationships between the different people living in South Africa developed over time. The area is the Orange River — or the Northern Frontier as it came to be called — a century after the arrival of the European settlers in the Cape. You will see what was happening between the people living there in about 1800, that is, at the end of the 18th Century.

UNIT 7

The struggle over land: The Northern Frontier

UNIT 7

The struggle over land: The Northern Frontier

South Africa is a very big country. It is about the same size as England, France, Spain and The Netherlands (Holland) put together. Because of this fact, it is not surprising that the shaping of the South Africa we know today was a complicated process. It took different forms in different parts of the country.

By the 18th Century (1700 – 1800), the main groups of people living in South Africa were the San, the Khoikhoi, African farmers and the Dutch. We have already seen in Unit 4 how the position of the San was weakened by the arrival of the Khoikhoi. Then in Unit 6, we saw how the arrival of the Dutch greatly weakened Khoikhoi society.

In the 17th Century, most of the action between the Khoikhoi and the Dutch took place in the south-western Cape. Things changed in the late 17th Century as some groups, for a number of different reasons, began to move northwards and eastwards away from the coast and into the interior of the country.

For most of the 18th Century, many parts of the country were not under the control of any one group. This was because groups operating in these areas were more or less equal in strength. When different groups met, they had to work out a way of getting along with one another. They had to decide about things like who could use the land, what items — like cattle or tobacco — they were prepared to exchange and what they wanted to get in return for these items. Often, they couldn't manage to do this peacefully and fights would break out.

But, before we look at the contact between different groups in more detail, let's think about the following idea.

Something to think about

Among the San, the idea of private property did not exist. This was because resources were scarce and sharing was necessary to ensure the survival of the band. Instead, there was a custom that if somebody in your band admired something you had, you gave it to them. This was a way of avoiding jealousy and preventing conflict. The custom ensured that, for example, the most beautiful knife might pass around many times and eventually come back to you.

How do we get what we need or want?

We all **need** certain things in order to stay alive. We also often **want** things that other people have. Most of us try to control this desire so that we can live peacefully with neighbours and friends. Sometimes, however, this desire leads to conflict.

UNIT 7

Exercise 1

Discuss these situations with a partner. Spend a few minutes on each one.

1. You have forgotten to bring lunch or money to school. It is breaktime and you feel desperately hungry. Two of your friends have just bought juicy hamburgers from the tuckshop. The smell alone is enough to drive you wild. What do you do?

2. All those in the athletics team are told that they need good running shoes. You go shopping with your mother that afternoon and buy a really nice pair. One of your friends comes to school the next day and tells you that she is dropping out of the athletics team because her parents can't afford to get her running shoes. What do you do?

3. Your family has an old VW Beetle. You can't help being affected by the images of all the luxurious new cars you see in the adverts on T.V. and at the movies. What a pleasure it would be to have one of those! List all the possible ways you could achieve this dream.

Which of the above situations arises from need and which from want? Does this make any difference to the action you would be prepared to take?

The Northern Frontier

An area of land that is not controlled by one group is called an **open frontier**. As soon as one group becomes dominant, the frontier becomes closed.

An interesting example of an open frontier is the area along the Orange river at the end of the 18th Century. You will see from the map on the next page that

UNIT 7

the groups operating in this area were the Khoisan*, the Tswana, the Dutch and the Oorlams*. As the Dutch, the Khoikhoi and the Oorlams moved further north, they came into contact with the San, the Tswana and other Khoikhoi groups already living along the Orange. This became the Northern Frontier or the area north of the Cape where, as yet, no one group dominated.

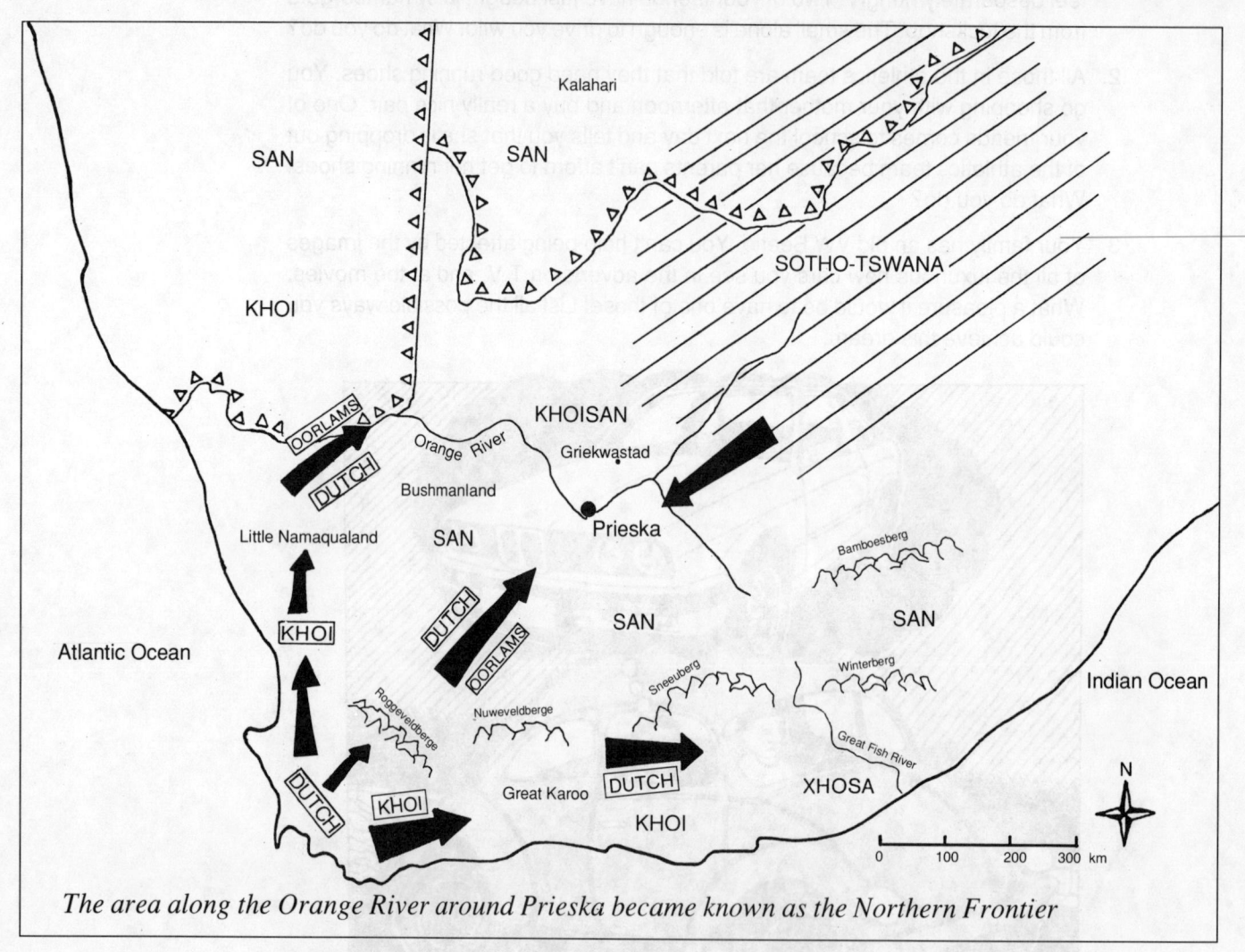

The area along the Orange River around Prieska became known as the Northern Frontier

This area remained an open frontier well into the 19th Century because of the harshness of the environment. It was a semi-desert area which was not suitable for crops. Having only one farm or grazing area was useless because most communities had to move regularly in search of water and grazing. Although important water sources were controlled, many people didn't register land in their names because they knew they would be moving on when the season changed.

New words

- Khoisan — the name given to communities that were made up of a mixture of San and Khoikhoi people. Because of the weakness of their position, the San and the Khoikhoi often joined forces to resist attacks by other groups.
- Oorlams — the name this book uses for people who were of mixed origin i.e. offspring from either the Dutch and the Khoikhoi, slaves and the Khoikhoi or the Dutch and slaves. The Oorlams formed a new cultural group in South Africa. As they were born

UNIT 7

and bred with the Dutch farmers, they could speak Dutch. They also followed many of the customs of the Dutch, especially the religious ones. They usually worked for the Dutch. They knew how to use horses and guns.

In the next section of this unit, we will look at what took place between these different groups on the Northern Frontier at the end of the 18th Century (in about the year 1800).

Come to the kgotla

The kgotla was a place in the town centre of a Tswana community where trading took place. It could be compared to a market in many respects. People liked to go to the kgotla at least once a month to exchange what they had for other things that they needed or wanted. The next exercise will give you some idea of how this trading worked.

A Tswana chief bringing ivory to sell

Exercise 2

Imagine that you are a member of one of the communities living along the Northern Frontier in 1800. You are sent to the kgotla to trade with people from other communities. The following role choices will give you information about what role you have to play i.e. who you are, what you have to exchange and what you would like to get.

Stage 1:

ROLE CHOICES

Divide into four groups to read and discuss your roles. Your teacher will give each group a number. Elect a member of your group to read aloud the role your group has to play. The rest of you follow in your book and ask the reader to stop if there is something you don't understand.

93

UNIT 7

Group 1

The Tswana   Date: 1800

You are Tswana people who hunt and farm cattle and sheep in the area. The chief of your village presides over the trading at the kgotla. His job is to settle any major fights but he usually doesn't interfere in regular trading.

You control the ivory trade since the greatest numbers of elephants are to be found in the area in which you live. Ivory is very precious because there is an export market for it and everybody wants it. This means that you can exchange it for almost anything you want.

You have fairly large herds of cattle. You know that the Dutch farmers who have come to the area will give you guns in exchange for cattle or ivory. And, more than anything else, you want guns! You have come to realise how impossible it is to defend yourselves against raids by the Dutch and the Oorlams using only your traditional weapons. This is one of the main reasons you are prepared to trade with the Dutch.

You also have karosses which you know the Dutch and the Oorlams will be interested in to keep out the winter cold.

An item you would like to get from the Dutch is a horse that you can use to patrol the area. But, you will have to play your cards carefully! From experience, you know that the Dutch are likely to trick you into trading with them for their useless objects. You are unimpressed by the looking-glasses, handkerchiefs and knives that they have. You think your knives are superior to theirs.

You also expect that the Dutch and the Oorlams will be trading tobacco and dagga, both of which you are eager to obtain. Although you grow some yourselves, the tobacco and dagga that the Dutch and the Oorlams have is much better than your own.

UNIT 7

You cultivate the land mainly to grow crops for your own use. You also obviously need land for grazing for your herds. However, the idea of owning land is foreign to you. That is, you do not believe that land can be traded or used to settle a debt. You definitely do not recognise the idea that land can simply be occupied. Only the chief has the right to give out land and to take it back. Everybody has the right to use the land though, it is true, some people have more land or better land than other people.

Here is a summary of the things you are interested in getting at the kgotla:
- More guns and gunpowder from the Dutch. You need these to protect yourselves from raiders and to carry out raids yourself.
- Tobacco and dagga from the Dutch or the Oorlams.
- 1 horse for transport.

Decide on a trading strategy i.e. work out what you want or need most before trading starts. Also, decide which group each of you will approach and how much you are prepared to "pay" for what you want.

Your teacher will give you the items you have to exchange. Divide them out among the members of your group. Every member must have at least one item to trade with.

Check that you have been given the right number of each item. You should have:

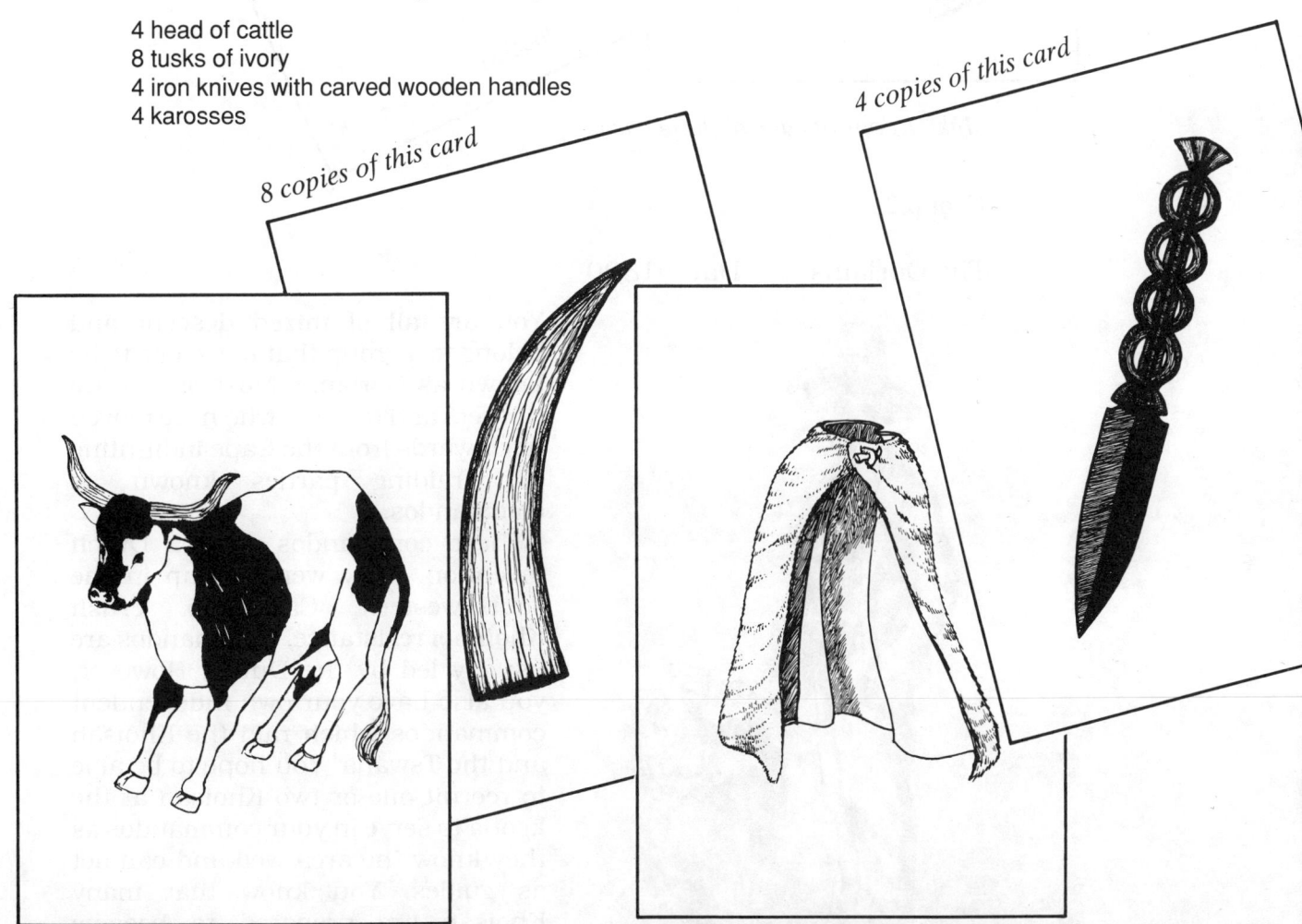

4 head of cattle
8 tusks of ivory
4 iron knives with carved wooden handles
4 karosses

8 copies of this card

4 copies of this card

4 copies of this card

4 copies of this card

UNIT 7

You also have a gun and some gunpowder to protect yourselves because occasionally trading has resulted in gun-battles. This gun is **not** for exchange. Decide which individual needs it most.

Gunpowder

Make 1 copy of each of these cards

Group 2

The Oorlams   Date: 1800

You are all of mixed descent and belong to a group that has come to be known as Oorlams. Most of you are hunters and traders, who have moved northwards from the Cape in hunting and raiding parties known as commandos.

These commandos were a Dutch invention. They were set up in the south-western Cape to crush Khoikhoi resistance. Commandos are usually led by the Dutch. However, you also have your own independent commandos which raid the Khoisan and the Tswana. You hope to be able to recruit one or two Khoisan at the kgotla to serve in your commandos as they know the area well and can act as guides. You know that many Khoisan are prepared to become labourers in exchange for guns and horses. You also hope to obtain cattle and sheep in exchange for your labour so that you can also be herders.

Many of you have acquired different skills. There are transport riders, small farmers, craftspeople and farm managers among you. Most of you are educated in Christianity and have learnt to sing psalms. Some of you have even learnt to read.

As some of you are also herders, you have cattle to exchange. You have obtained these mainly from raids on the Khoisan and occasionally on the Tswana. This is a good area for stock-farming and you know that the Dutch are very keen to acquire more cattle. You hope to sell some cattle to the Dutch in exchange for guns.

You also have tobacco and dagga which are enjoyed very much by the Khoisan and the Tswana. Although they grow both themselves, the quality of their crop is not nearly as good as what you have to sell.

You feel strongly that Dutch farmers shouldn't sell guns to the Tswana community as this would strenghten their position and make it more difficult for you to get what you want out of them.

You very much want to get ivory from the Tswana. You are busy setting up a system for selling ivory directly to Cape Town without using Dutch farmers as agents. This means that your profits will be greater. You therefore have an interest in keeping a good relationship with the Tswana community to ensure that they supply you with ivory.

In addition, you like to be seen to be creating stable relationships in the area. This may ensure that the Dutch authorities will recognise the land claims you make. Like the Dutch, you try to claim areas of land for yourself and then register your ownership of that land with the authorities of the Company in Cape Town.

Here is a summary of the things you are interested in obtaining at the kgotla:
- More guns and gunpowder from the Dutch farmers. You know that the Dutch are willing to trade in guns. (The Company in Cape Town has declared this illegal but trading in guns happens all the time.)
- A Khoisan labourer to act as a guide which you know will cost you a gun and gunpowder.
- As much ivory as possible from the Tswana, possibly in exchange for sheep, tobacco and dagga.
- 3 head of cattle from the Khoisan or the Tswana to exchange later on for guns and gunpowder.
- 2 iron knives from the Tswana or the Dutch for hunting and cooking.
- 2 karosses from the Khoisan or the Tswana.

Decide on a trading strategy i.e. work out what you want or need most before trading starts. Also, decide which group each of you will approach and how much you are prepared to "pay" for what you want.

Your teacher will give you the items you have to exchange. Divide them out among the members of your group. Every member must have at least one item to trade with.

Check that you have been given the right number of each item. You should have:

1 gun and some gunpowder
3 head of cattle
1 horse
6 pouches of tobacco
8 bags of dagga

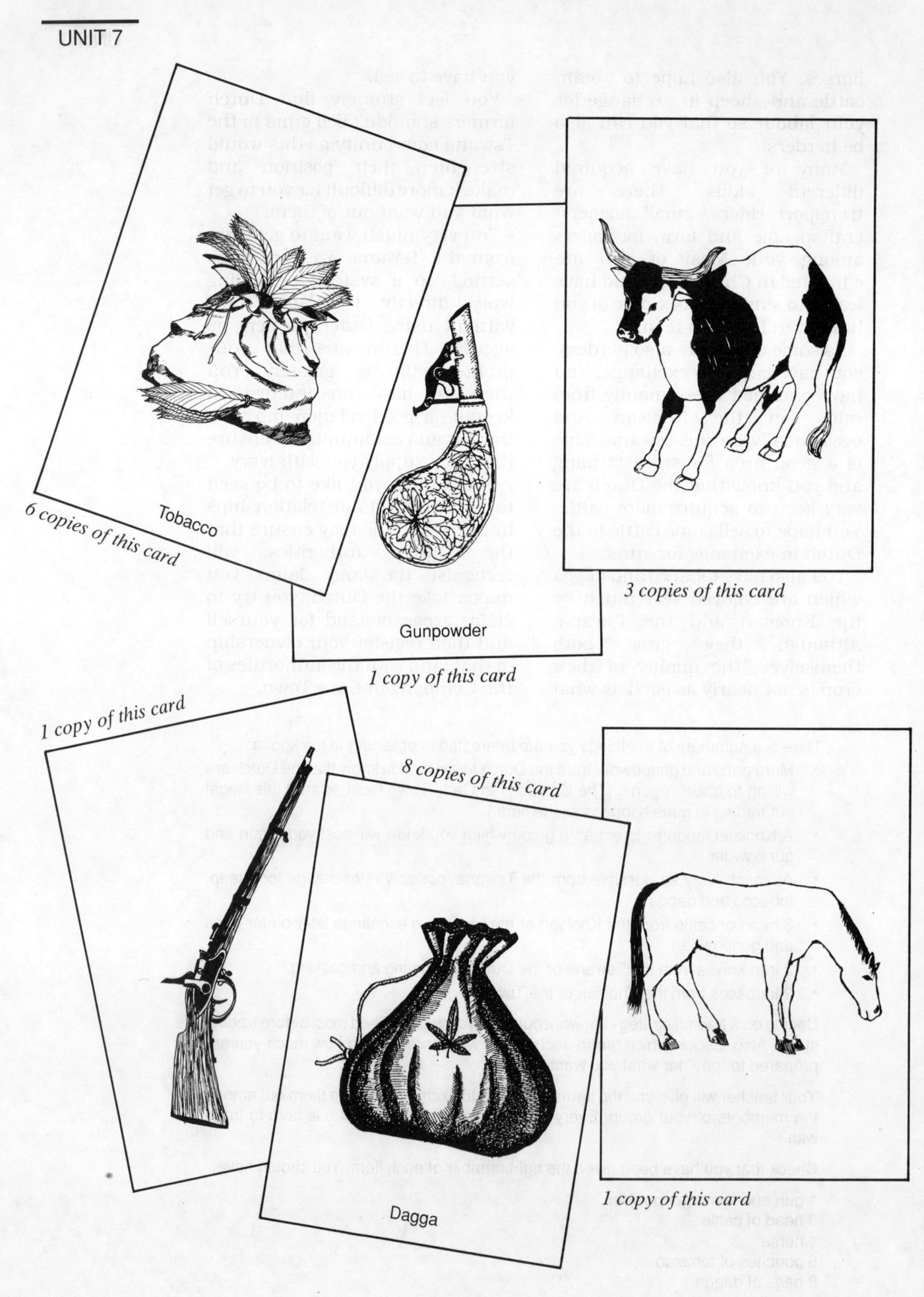

UNIT 7

Tobacco — 6 copies of this card

Gunpowder — 1 copy of this card

3 copies of this card

1 copy of this card

8 copies of this card

Dagga

1 copy of this card

98

UNIT 7

You also have 3 guns and gunpowder to protect yourselves because trading has sometimes resulted in gun-battles. These are **not** for exchange. Decide which individuals need them most. You plan to trade peacefully but if absolutely necessary you are prepared to take what you want by force.

3 copies of this card

Gunpowder

3 copies of this card

Group 3

The Khoisan   Date: 1800

UNIT 7

You are members of the Khoisan community. As the name suggests, some of you are of San descent and some are of Khoikhoi origin. Some of you have retreated from the Cape as life became too difficult for you. You live in between Tswana settlements where most of you still practise a hunter-gathering lifestyle. Some of you have sheep and cattle.

The arrival of Dutch farmers and the Oorlams have made you the poorest community in the area. The Dutch and the Oorlams have guns! This makes it easy for them to raid your settlements, steal your cattle and, in some cases, force you off your land or make you become labourers.

The constant raids you have suffered have weakened your position so much that you are prepared to do almost anything to obtain guns. You hope to use these to carry out counter-raids or simply to defend yourselves from being raided. But, obtaining guns usually means being labourers in the commandos of the Dutch or the Oorlams. These are groups especially set up for the purpose of raiding the Tswana and yourselves. This means that some of you have, on occasion, raided your own people. Sometimes you do manage to get guns in exchange for working as shepherds and herders for the Dutch or the Oorlams.

You also produce karosses from wild animal skins which you know the Dutch and the Oorlams are interested in buying. They want these for their own use and also to export. You generally exchange these for things like tobacco and dagga. Although you do grow some of your own, the tobacco and dagga which the Dutch and the Oorlams have is much better than your own. Though the Dutch try to impress you with their linen handkerchiefs, you are not interested in these strange objects.

Like the Tswana, you believe that all the members of your community have the right to use the land and that nobody can own it. You have been forced to change your nomadic lifestyle as you realise that it is not wise to move around too much when so many different groups are competing for the land in the area. Also, mainly the Dutch, but sometimes the Oorlams too, claim whatever land they can and then register it as theirs with the Company officials in Cape Town.

One effect of their occupation of land in the area is that you are being squeezed off the land you are using. This is bringing you into conflict with the Tswana with whom you have generally had good relations.

Here is a summary of the things you are interested in getting at the kgotla:
- Some guns and gunpowder from the Dutch or the Oorlams to ensure that you can defend yourselves against their raids.
- 2 head of cattle from the Dutch, the Tswana or the Oorlams to make up for the ones that have been stolen from you.
- Dagga or tobacco from the Oorlams or the Dutch.
- 1 horse for you to ride around the area where you live to keep a check on things.
- 1 dog which you know the Dutch will be willing to exchange for a kaross.
- 1 iron knife from the Tswana or the Dutch.

Decide on a trading strategy i.e. decide what you want or need most before trading starts. Also, decide which group each of you will approach and how much you are prepared to "pay" for what you want.

UNIT 7

Your teacher will give you the items you have to exchange. Divide them out among the members of your group. Every member must have at least one item to trade with.

Check that you have been given the right number of each item. You should have:

1 head of cattle
3 karosses
3 people who are prepared to
become labourers for a while

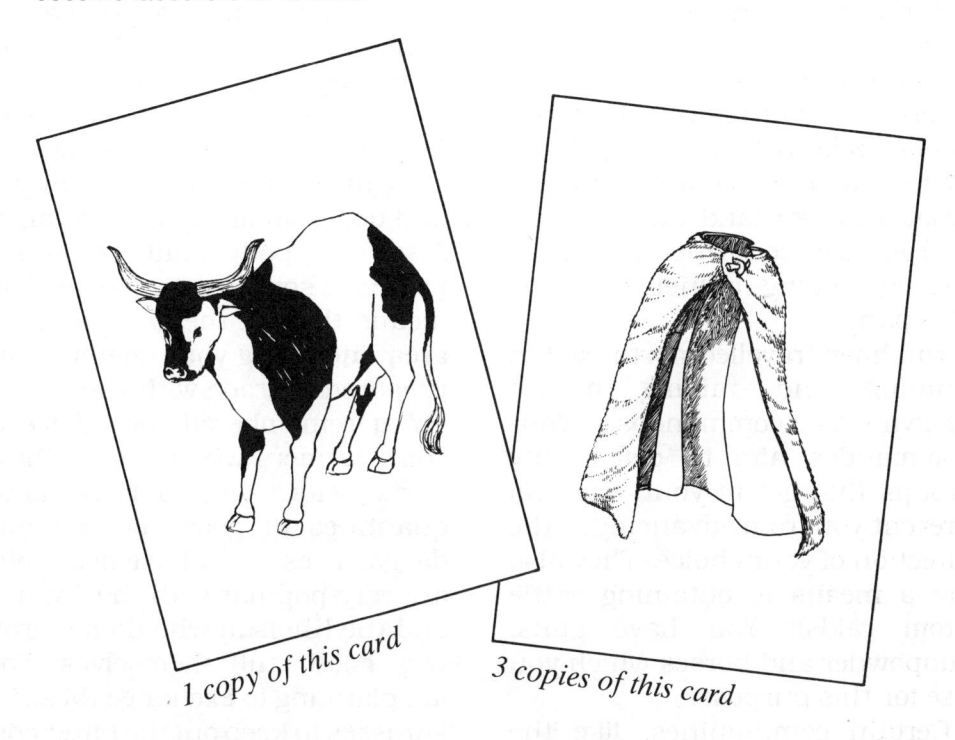

1 copy of this card

3 copies of this card

Be careful! You have no guns to protect yourself with and you can remember times when unsuccessful trading has resulted in gun-battles.

Group 4

The Dutch   Date: 1800

101

UNIT 7

You are Dutch farmers who left the south-western Cape because you realised that your opportunities there were limited. Though your main interest has been crop-farming, you realise that you won't be able to grow much in this harsh environment. You keep cattle and would like to acquire more.

You were attracted to the Cape interior as you realised that you could make a better living here. There is less competition for resources like land and animals and you can be further away from the controlling influence of the Company.

You have travelled north-east in hunting and raiding parties known as commandos. Your commandos aim to defeat any groups that get in your way and prevent you from advancing in the direction of your choice. They also are a means of obtaining cattle (from raids)! You have guns, gunpowder and horses which you use for this purpose.

Certain communities, like the Khoisan and some of the Tswana, are unlikely to attack you because the majority of them don't have any guns. This means you have been able to force some of them to trade with you or you have raided their villages and stolen their cattle. On occasion, you have even captured Khoisan women and children and used them as slaves.

According to Company law, it is illegal to trade in guns. However, you know that you can get away with it. Some Khoisan and Oorlams are prepared to participate in your commandos in exchange for guns and gunpowder. You have even heard of cases where the Khoisan have participated in raids on their own people. Since they know the area much better than you do, they can be of great use to you as guides.

You have already made some enemies in the area by occupying land that some Tswana and Khoisan groups claim is theirs. They think that land belongs to them because they use it. They don't understand that you have to register your claims with the Company in Cape Town before you can say land belongs to you. And, in any case, the Company only recognises the claims made by you and occasionally by the Oorlams. Also, everybody wants guns and you have some for exchange. This means that all the groups in the area, including your enemies, are prepared to trade with you.

You remembered the advice of some farmers who came to these parts before you to bring large quantities of good tobacco and dagga. These, you have been told, are very popular with the Tswana and the Khoisan who do not grow very good stuff themselves. You are planning to exchange these for karosses to keep out the bitter cold in winter. You may even be able to get cattle in exchange for dagga. Because the area is difficult to farm crops in, you are quite keen to increase the size of your herds and become stock-farmers.

You also think that the Khoisan and the Tswana will be impressed with your iron knives and linen handkerchiefs.

There is a good trade in ivory between the Tswana in this area and the Company for which you act as middlemen or agents. For this reason, you are eager to buy as much ivory from the Tswana as possible. You know that the Oorlams are trying to get in on this trade, so you hope to buy up whatever ivory is available before they do.

UNIT 7

Here is a summary of the things you are interested in obtaining at the kgotla:
- 3 Khoisan labourers which you know are likely to cost you a gun and some gunpowder each.
- As much ivory as possible from the Tswana - they are very keen to get tobacco and dagga from you, as well as a horse.
- 7 head of cattle from the Khoisan, the Tswana or the Oorlams.
- 4 karosses from the Khoisan or the Tswana.

Decide on a trading strategy i.e. work out what you want or need most before trading starts. Also, decide which group each of you will approach and how much you are prepared to "pay" for what you want.

Your teacher will give you the items you have to exchange. Divide them out among the members of your group. Every person in the group must have at least one item to trade with.

Check that you have been given the right number of each item. You should have:

4 guns and gunpowder
2 horses
15 pouches of tobacco
20 bags of dagga
2 dogs
4 linen handkerchiefs
4 iron knives

4 copies of this card

4 copies of this card
Gunpowder

4 copies of this card

2 copies of this card

20 copies of this card

15 copies of this card
Tobacco

2 copies of this card

4 copies of this card

103

UNIT 7

You have brought 6 guns with you for protection as you have heard that trading at the kgotla has sometimes resulted in gun-battles. These guns are **not** for exchange. Decide which individuals are most likely to need them. You plan to trade peacefully but if necessary you are prepared to take what you want by force.

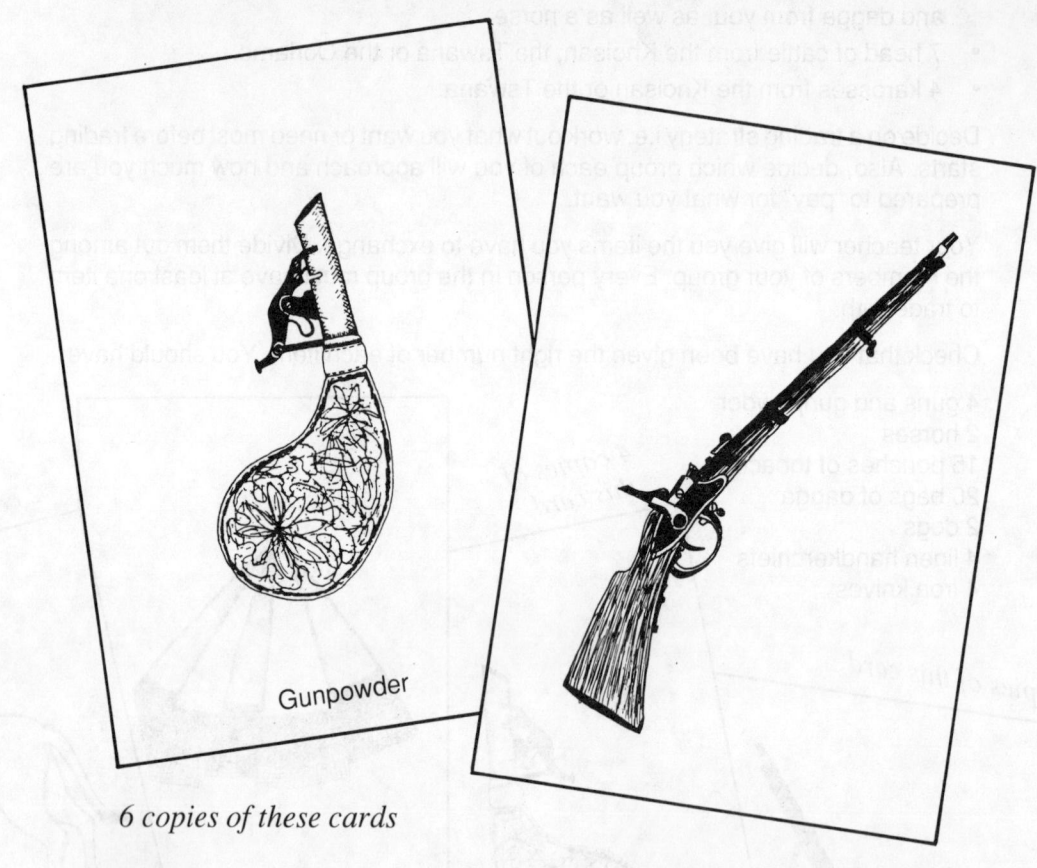

Gunpowder

6 copies of these cards

Stage 2:

PREPARING FOR TRADING

1. Your teacher will give you labels on which you must write what group you belong to e.g. Khoisan, Dutch etc. This will tell you with whom you are dealing once trading starts.

2. Most people believe very strongly that killing is wrong. So, if you have a gun, think very carefully before you show it. You may start a gun-battle in which people could lose their lives. You could also destroy the possibility of future trade with a particular group in the area.

There are **3 Rules** about using guns that those who have guns have to follow to stay in the game:

a. If somebody points a gun at you and you point one back at them, you are even. Neither of you has lost or gained anything.

b. If someone points a gun at you and you don't have one to point back, you have to hand over any item that you have and he/she wants.

c. You cannot take a Khoisan labourer by force. Labourers that are taken by force prove to be unreliable because they usually run away. You can only obtain a labourer through a proper system of exchange. The Khoisan expect payment for their labour. They are not slaves.

3. Now go to the kgotla and see if you can get what you planned to get in exchange for the item/s you have. You may have to approach more than one group for the same item e.g. if you are a Dutch farmer and you want cattle, you could approach the Tswana, the Khoisan or the Oorlams as you know that they are all likely to have cattle for exchange.

How well did you trade?

Trading always has an effect on the way different groups of people relate to each other. To summarise what you have learnt about the relationships between the different groups of people along the Northern Frontier in 1800, do this exercise.

Exercise 3

Work in the same groups as the ones you were put into for the role-play.

1. Elect a member of your group to give a reportback.

2. Together prepare this reportback. It should cover the following areas:
   a. what your group hoped to get
   b. what your group had to exchange
   c. what your group managed to get
   d. why your group managed to get these items.

3. Now each group will have a turn to reportback to the whole class. After each reportback, members of each group will be given a chance to add anything important they think has been left out. Other groups will be given a chance to ask questions.

4. To end with, there will be a whole class discussion during which you will be able to comment on anything about the game that you found interesting.

Different attitudes to land

Although land wasn't something that people traded for as such, it was something that all groups needed and wanted. Being clear about what the **different attitudes to land** of these four groups of people were, will help you to understand the struggles over the land that were to follow later in most parts of the country.

Exercise 4

Now read through all four role choices and draw up a table in which you summarise, in point form, the **different attitudes to land** of each of these four groups. Do this in the following way:

UNIT 7

DIFFERENT ATTITUDES TO LAND			
TSWANA	OORLAMS	KHOISAN	DUTCH FARMERS
• Everybody has the right to use the land to grow crops and graze cattle. • Only the chief has the right to give out land and take it back. • Some people have more land or better land than other people. • You can't own land i.e. land can't be traded or used for paying a debt. • You can't occupy land that other people are using.			

Something to think about

Some people argue that those who have guns will always triumph over those who do not. South Africa has generally been a very violent society and continues to be so. What do you think about the idea of using violence to get what you need or want?

UNIT 7

Summing up

The main ideas you learned about in this unit are:

1. An area of land that is not controlled by one group is called an **open frontier**. As soon as one group becomes dominant, the frontier becomes closed.

2. The Northern Frontier (see map on p 92) remained an open frontier well into the 19th Century because of the harshness of the environment.

3. Trading took place between the Tswana, the Oorlams, the Khoisan and the Dutch on the Nothern Frontier.

4. Groups who had greater wealth were in a stronger position to trade than those who were poorer.

5. Groups who had guns were in a stronger position to trade than those who didn't.

The battle-lines became more clearly drawn in the 19th Century when indigenous societies found themselves fighting against both the British and the Boers. The next unit examines how the southern Sotho lost land on which they lived through the actions of the British.

UNIT 8

The struggle over land: The Basotho lose out

UNIT 8

The struggle over land: The Basotho lose out

The previous unit gave you some idea about what was happening between the Tswana, the Oorlams, the Khoisan and the Dutch on the Northern Frontier at the end of the 18th Century. Because it was still an **open** frontier, no one group was in control.

In this unit, we will study what happened on another **open** frontier. This time we look at the rise of the Basotho kingdom in the 19th Century. The main groups of people involved in this episode were the Basotho, the Boers and the British. Of these, the British, who had taken over the Cape from the Dutch in 1795, were the most powerful group. This was because they were backed by Britain who could provide them with a well-organised and well-equipped army. It was the presence of the British that resulted in the **closing** of this frontier: they paved the way for the Boers to establish their control over what came to be called the Orange Free State. The Orange Free State included land which had previously been part of the Basotho kingdom.

The story of the closing of this frontier is the story of how the Basotho lost the use of most of their fertile land. It is not a unique story. It is similar to what happened, during the course of the 19th century, to other major African kingdoms in the country, like the Xhosa, the Zulu and the Pedi.

The Basotho kingdom today — Lesotho

Before we find out about the Basotho kingdom in the 19th Century, let's see what we know about what remains of it today.

Exercise 1

Look at this map of southern Africa. Then discuss these questions as a class.

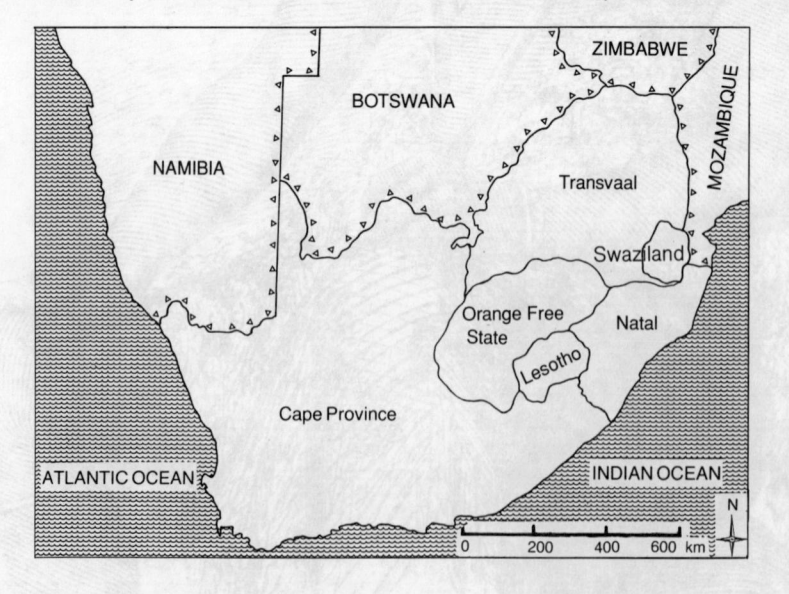

UNIT 8

1. Where is Lesotho?
2. In what direction would you need to travel to get to Lesotho from
    a. Durban?
    b. Johannesburg?
    c. Cape Town?
    d. where you live?
3. Approximately how big is Lesotho?
4. What do you know about Lesotho?

The story of the Basotho in the 19th Century

The Basotho kingdom at one time included what is today part of the Orange Free State and Lesotho. You will see how the Basotho lost a great deal of land to the Boers and how Britain finally took over the Basotho kingdom in 1868.

Much of the story that follows is a summary from a classroom pack called **The land the Basotho lost** produced by Sached, an organisation that aims to produce democratic education materials. This pack tells of the rise and survival of the Basotho kingdom between 1820 and 1871.

Exercise 2

To find out how the Basotho lost a large part of their land, read this information and look carefully at the maps that go with it. Try to read between the lines i.e. ask yourself questions about what you are reading. Does the information that follows provide answers? To help you, there are some questions to think about in the margins. They are shown by this symbol:

The rise of the Basotho state

By 1820, most people living in the area just north of the Orange River belonged to one of 3 main Sotho groups — the Fokeng, the Koena or the Tlokoa. Each group consisted of a number of chiefdoms, each under the leadership of a chief.

During the next 20 years, this situation changed a great deal. By 1840, a man called Moshoeshoe, the leader of a small chiefdom, had managed to bring the Fokeng and the Koena chiefdoms under his control and to build them into a strong state. He had become so important that he was addressed as **Morena oa Basotho** (Chief of the Basotho).

Moshoeshoe was able to bring the Fokeng and the Koena under his control. They became part of his kingdom. The Tlokoa remained independent until they were defeated by Moshoeshoe in 1853.

111

UNIT 8

Pressures from all sides

Moshoeshoe's people were not isolated. The diagram below shows that there were many other groups of people living in the area in the 1830s. All these people influenced each other's lives in some way.

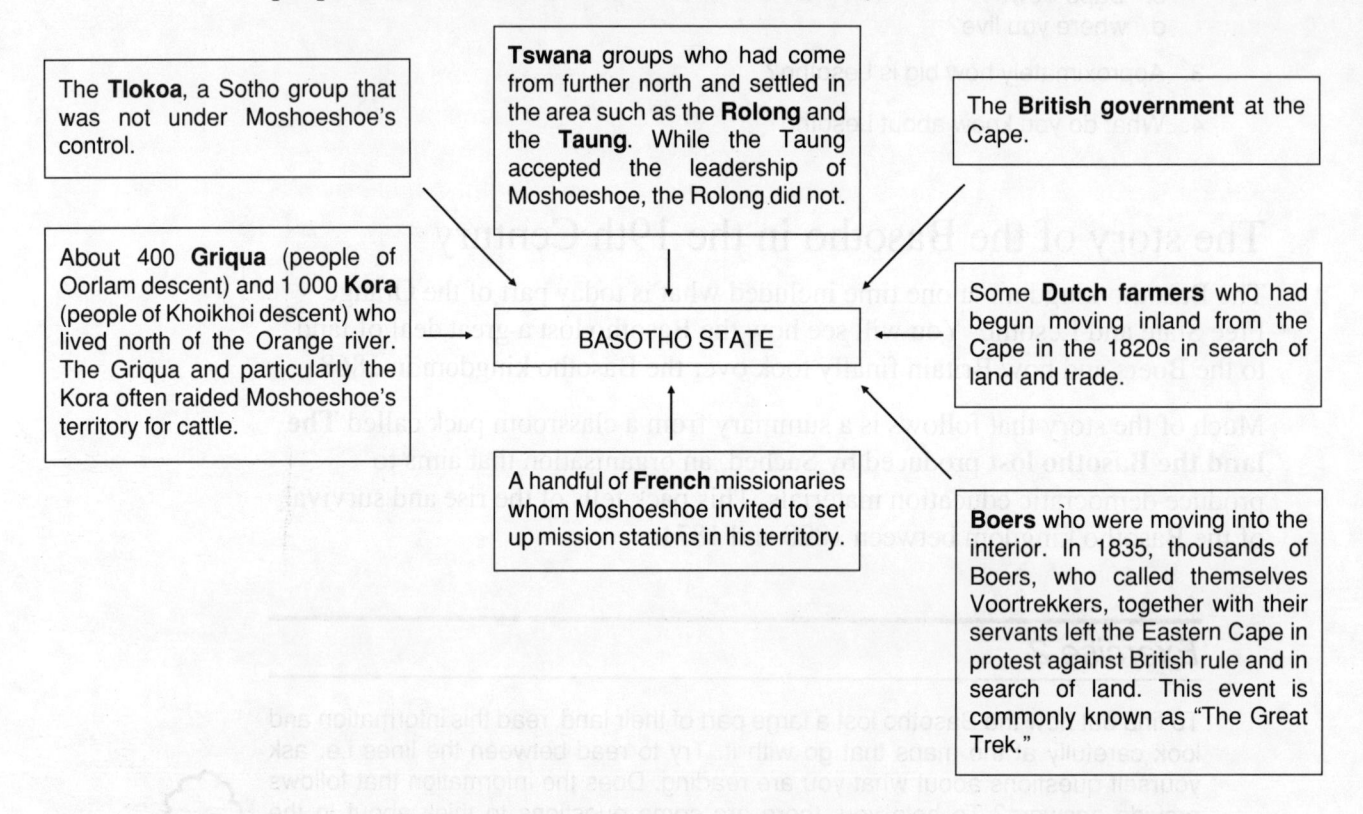

- The **Tlokoa**, a Sotho group that was not under Moshoeshoe's control.

- **Tswana** groups who had come from further north and settled in the area such as the **Rolong** and the **Taung**. While the Taung accepted the leadership of Moshoeshoe, the Rolong did not.

- The **British government** at the Cape.

- About 400 **Griqua** (people of Oorlam descent) and 1 000 **Kora** (people of Khoikhoi descent) who lived north of the Orange river. The Griqua and particularly the Kora often raided Moshoeshoe's territory for cattle.

- **BASOTHO STATE**

- Some **Dutch farmers** who had begun moving inland from the Cape in the 1820s in search of land and trade.

- A handful of **French** missionaries whom Moshoeshoe invited to set up mission stations in his territory.

- **Boers** who were moving into the interior. In 1835, thousands of Boers, who called themselves Voortrekkers, together with their servants left the Eastern Cape in protest against British rule and in search of land. This event is commonly known as "The Great Trek."

The Basotho kingdom and its neighbours in the 1830s

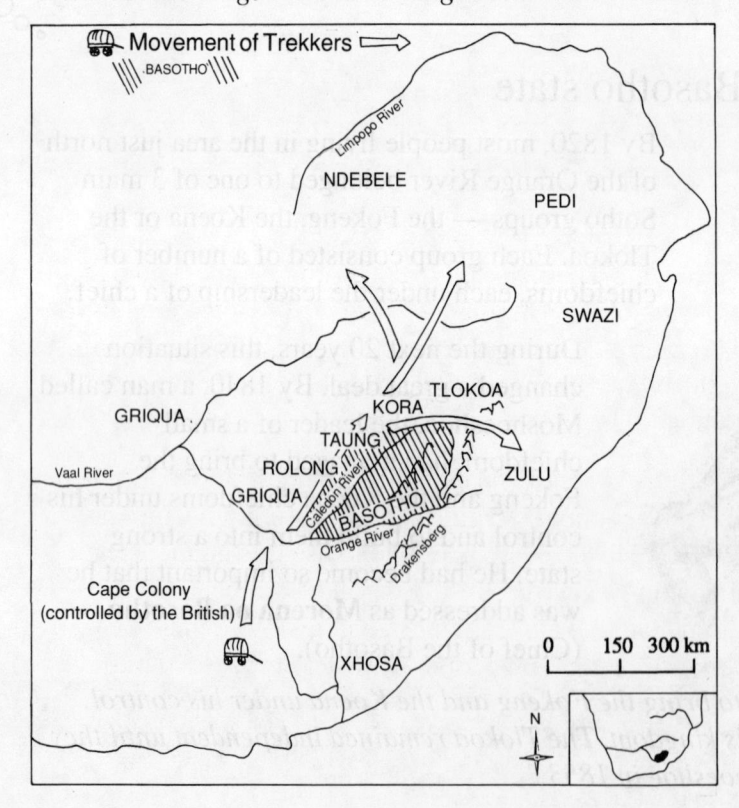

112

Moshoeshoe moves to Thaba Bosiu

The 1820s and 1830s were a time of great upheaval. There were **many wars about land** which caused thousands of people to flee to other parts of the country. For example, the Tlokoa were driven from their villages and, in turn, attacked other settlements in the area.

Moshoeshoe realised that his people needed a stronger fortress to protect themselves from attack. He very wisely chose a flat-topped mountain surrounded by a fertile plain for his new capital. Because they arrived there at night, it was called Thaba Bosiu which means the Mountain of the Night. Over the next 50 years, many people attacked this mountain stronghold. No one ever succeeded in conquering it.

Thaba Bosiu — Mountain of the Night

How Moshoeshoe built up his power

Moshoeshoe built up his power at Thaba Bosiu by attracting people who had been unsettled by the land wars of the 1820s and 1830s. They were given **land** and were **lent** cattle and, in return, Moshoeshoe expected them to support him and his people in war. In this way, Moshoeshoe built up his chiefdom from 25 000 people in 1836 to 80 000 in 1848.

Moshoeshoe also used a **tribute** system. His supporters paid tribute to him by working for a time on his fields without pay or by giving him grain from the land they farmed. In the 1830s Moshoeshoe was able to use this grain, as well as cattle obtained from raids on weaker groups, to buy large numbers of guns and horses from British traders and from some missionaries. With these he could protect his followers from attack by people who were moving into the area.

UNIT 8

Trouble over the land

By the mid-1830s, Moshoeshoe's chiefdom had spread from Thaba Bosiu over a wide area and had grown into the largest and most powerful chiefdom in the region.

The land that the Basotho occupied was mountainous and had few fertile areas. The most fertile part was the Caledon River Valley. The Basotho used this valley for growing crops and keeping livestock. Grain could be grown without irrigation. Cattle and large herds of game grazed on the thick grass in the area. It was into this fertile valley that the Boers moved.

The Caledon River Valley, the most fertile area of the Basotho Kingdom

> What should Moshoeshoe do? If the Boers were after the Basotho's best land, maybe he should try to get help from the British? After all, the British wanted peace in the region to protect their trade . . .

At first, the Boers and the Basotho lived peacefully with each other in the Caledon Valley. They relied on each other. Trading between the Basotho and the Boers increased: in exchange for grain and cattle, the Basotho got large stores of guns and gunpowder from the Boers. Some of these Boers saw themselves as friends or even subjects of Moshoeshoe.

However, by the end of the 1830s, the Basotho Kingdom, other African groups and some of the Boers all wanted control of the Caledon River Valley because it was so fertile. Moshoeshoe did not want to lose the use of any of this land to the Boers. He also did not want to go to war against them.

By now Moshoeshoe had already become aware of the power of the British in southern Africa. He had heard how the British had defeated the Xhosa on the Cape Eastern Frontier.

UNIT 8

The first boundary line

In 1843 Napier, who was the Cape Governor, and Moshoeshoe signed a **treaty of friendship** which drew boundaries around Moshoeshoe's territory.

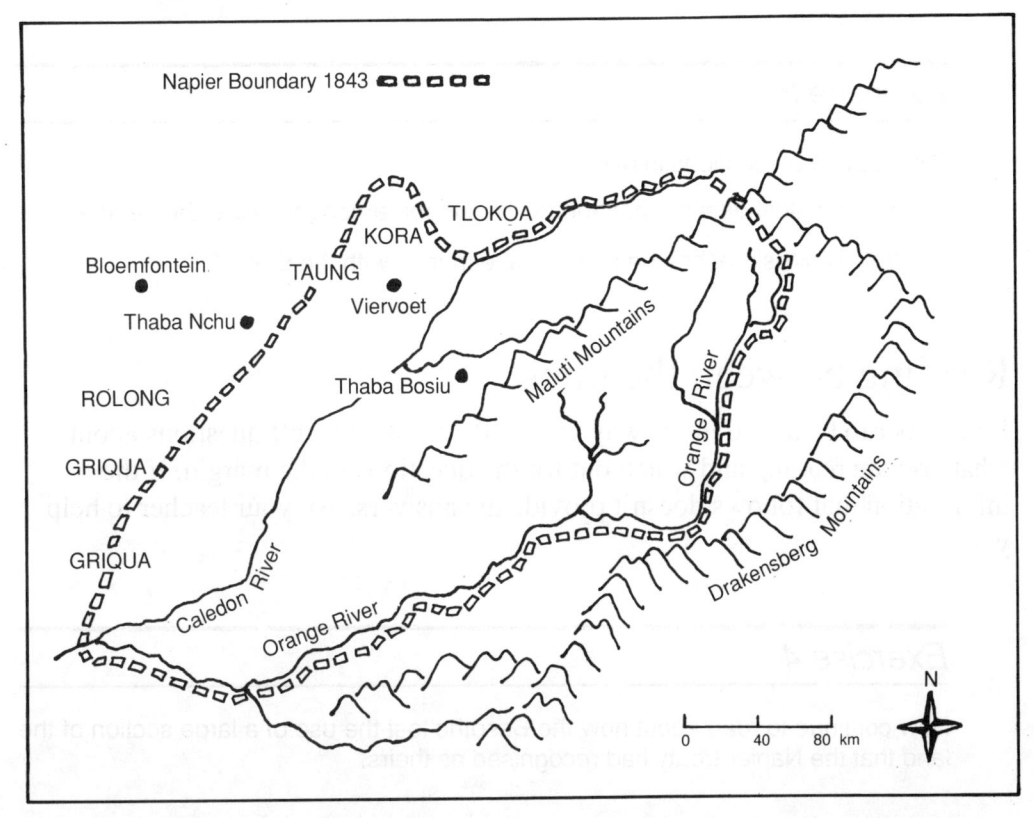

The Napier treaty recognised most of the territory that Moshoeshoe claimed. It included land occupied by the Rolong, the Taung, the Kora, the Tlokoa and the Boers. The problem was that neither the Rolong, the Tlokoa nor most of the Boers were prepared to accept Moshoeshoe's authority. And so what next?

Napier hoped that this treaty would keep peace in the area so that British trade could carry on undisturbed.

Moshoeshoe hoped that this treaty would control the number of Boers living on his land.

115

UNIT 8

How well did you read?

Take a quick break from all this reading to check how much you can remember.

Exercise 3

Discuss these questions in pairs.

1. How did Moshoeshoe manage to win support among the Basotho people?
2. Why did Moshoeshoe decide to make friends with the British?

Reading between the lines

Remember to be active in the way you read i.e. ask yourself questions about what you are reading and watch out for the questions in the margin. If the information that follows doesn't provide the answers, ask your teacher to help you.

Exercise 4

Now continue to read about how the Basotho lost the use of a large section of the land that the Napier treaty had recognised as theirs.

The boers gain land

Some Boers thought they owned the land they occupied. But, as one of Moshoeshoe's sons explained:

It is like letting people sit on chairs when they enter your house. They may sit down, but the chairs do not belong to them.

To avoid conflict with the Boers, Moshoeshoe finally agreed to make a section of Basotho land in the triangle between the Orange and the Caledon rivers available to the Boers. The Boers could rent — **but not buy** — this land.

Moshoeshoe agreed to this in the hope that his people would be protected against losing more land to the Boers. However, this agreement didn't satisfy everybody.

> What if the Boers thought that the piece of land available to them was too small? What if lesser Basotho chiefs wondered why Moshoeshoe was making space for strangers? They couldn't let strangers take their best land . . .

Conflict between the Basotho and the British

Tensions increased between the Basotho and some of the Boers over the Caledon River Valley. And, on the north-west border, Moshoeshoe was having problems with the Rolong who still would not accept his authority.

The Governor of the Cape at the time was a man called Harry Smith. His solution was to proclaim British control over all the Basotho territory in 1848: African chiefs in the area would continue to rule over their own chiefdoms and the Boers and the British would be ruled by British magistrates. The Boers would then become British subjects and would hopefully bring stability to the area. Not surprisingly, this step greatly angered the Voortrekkers — they had left the Cape Colony precisely because they did not want to be ruled by the British.

In 1850, Warden, the British magistrate who was put in control of the Caledon River Valley, stated his concern that the Basotho kingdom was becoming too powerful.

In 1851, with Smith's consent, Warden sent an army of British troops, Griqua, Kora, Rolong and a small number of Boers to attack the Basotho. At this stage, many of the Boers preferred to trade with the Basotho rather than go to war with them. The Basotho defeated Warden's army at Viervoet. (See map on page 115). The next year the British led another attack against the Basotho and again they were defeated. This shows the strength of the Basotho at this time.

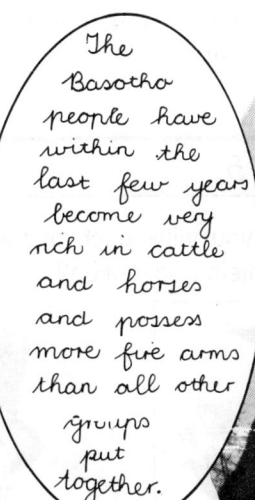

The Basotho people have within the last few years become very rich in cattle and horses and possess more fire arms than all other groups put together.

The birth of the Orange Free State

After suffering these defeats, both Harry Smith and Warden lost their jobs. The new governor of the Cape, George Cathcart, believed that it would be best for Britain to withdraw from the area. His reasons were that

- involvement in the region was costing too much financially
- the Boers were threatening to side with Moshoeshoe against the British unless the British recognised their independence in the areas north of the Cape
- Britain did not want a war against both the Boers and the Basotho.

So, what do you think happened next?

The Basotho had fought and beaten the British twice. Why did Moshoeshoe still want to be friendly with them? Perhaps he hoped that they would help keep the Boers under control . . . Why did the Boers threaten to side with Moshoeshoe? Perhaps then the British would stop telling them what to do . . .

UNIT 8

As Moshoeshoe had feared all along, the British and some of the Boers got together. They held a convention or great meeting in Bloemfontein in 1854. At the Bloemfontein Convention, the British recognised the independence of the Boers in the area between the Orange and the Vaal rivers. This gave rise to the independent Boer Republic of the Orange Free State. No African chiefdoms were consulted. The Bloemfontein Convention made no reference to Moshoeshoe and did not state what the boundaries between the Basotho kingdom and the OFS were. This was to cause conflict in years to come.

Check your understanding

Do the following exercise with a partner to make sure you are thinking clearly about all these events.

Exercise 5

1. How do you think each of the following people would have reacted to the Bloemfontein Convention?

- A Voortrekker leader
- Moshoeshoe
- George Cathcart, the Governor of the Cape

The final stage of this struggle

This is the last episode of this story of the Basotho.

Exercise 6

Read about a further loss of land for the Basotho - this happened as a result of the military support the Boers received from the British.

The tension mounts

By the time the Orange Free State was established, Moshoeshoe was at the height of his power. Remember, he had defeated the Tlokoa in 1853. There were now about 100 000 people under his control. This included all the major African groups in the area except for the Rolong.

118

Soon after 1854, the Basotho started taking cattle and horses from Boer farms. The Boers called this stock theft, but the chiefs on the frontier thought that they had a right to take Boer stock. As one of the thiefs said:

> They have taken away my country and those who have done it must feed me.

Tension between the Basotho and the OFS increased. The Basotho argued that Boer complaints were exaggerated because they were looking for an excuse to declare war on the Basotho. Moshoeshoe himself said:

Believe me, the real cause of the dispute is the ground. They wish to drive my people out.

However, Moshoeshoe did not want war with the OFS. He was always afraid that the British would side with the OFS in a war.

War against the OFS

In March 1858, the OFS declared war on the Basotho kingdom. The British came to their aid by supplying them with weapons. The Boers were also helped in this war by Moshoeshoe's old enemies, the Tlokoa.

The Boer forces advanced, attacking and looting villages as they went along. At the same time, Moshoeshoe's soldiers attacked Boer farms, taking livestock and burning homesteads. When this news reached the Boers, many of them returned home.

UNIT 8

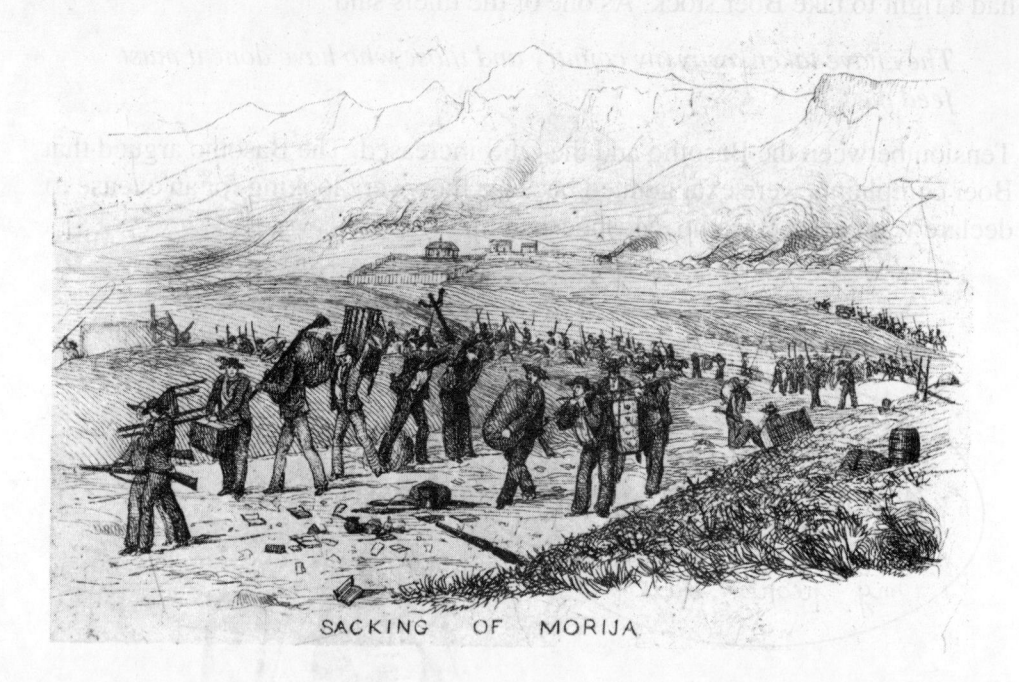

SACKING OF MORIJA

Why should the Basotho have to give up more land? After all, they had won the war...

By September, the OFS had been defeated and a peace treaty was signed. Moshoeshoe agreed that the governor of the Cape should be called in to settle the peace. Because Moshoeshoe still wanted to keep Britain on his side, he agreed to losing more land to the OFS. Many of the Basotho chiefs were not convinced that this was the right thing to do.

The OFS gains strength

The 1858 war showed that the Basotho people were strong enough to defend themselves against the Boers. The OFS, on the other hand, was weak.

But, for many reasons, the OFS grew stronger in the 1860s. One reason was that the OFS government was able to import large numbers of weapons, including cannons from the British in the Cape.

At the same time, Moshoeshoe's control over his kingdom grew weaker. One reason for this was that it was more difficult to get weapons because Britain refused to allow the sale of weapons to African kingdoms after 1854.

A long and bitter war broke out between the OFS and the Basotho in 1865. The Basotho called it the **War of Cannon's Boom**. The OFS claimed that the war was about cattle but it was really about land. Although the Basotho were suffering greatly, the Boers were not able to defeat them. All the while, Moshoeshoe still hoped that Britain would come to his aid.

UNIT 8

The British rule over "Basutoland"

Moshoeshoe knew that his people could not go on and on fighting the Boers. But, he also knew that he could not just give up his land and his people to them. He realised that the only possibility of keeping any of his land was to bring it under British control.

After a number of appeals from Moshoeshoe, the British finally agreed to take over the Basotho kingdom in 1868. It became known as "Basutoland" and all the Basotho people became British subjects.

A treaty between "Basutoland" and the OFS was signed in February 1869. The map opposite shows the final border settlement between "Basutoland" and the OFS and this is still the border of Lesotho today.

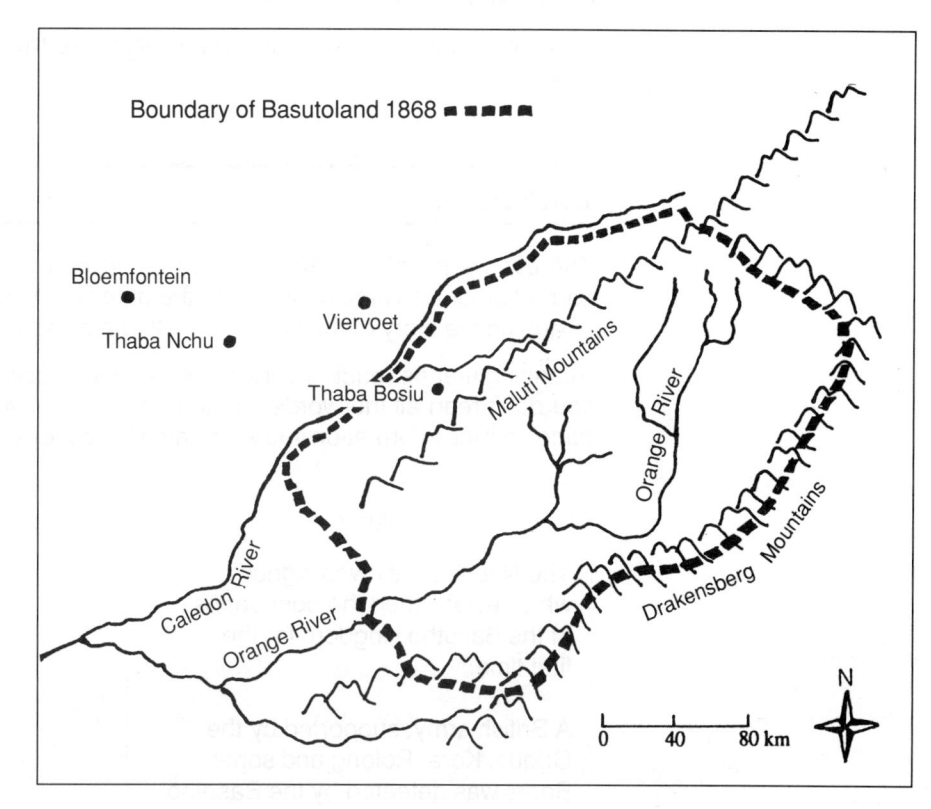

Boundary of Basutoland 1868 ▪ ▪ ▪ ▪ ▪

I am dissatisfied. I have been covered with shame, and I feel great grief... I was never consulted. I am only left with a small part of my country which is overcrowded with people.

121

UNIT 8

The Basotho kingdom lost most of its fertile land to the Boers. But, under the very able leadership of Moshoeshoe, it survived the kind of pressures which destroyed other African kingdoms.

What happened when?

The next two exercises will help you to organise the information you have just read.

Exercise 7

The events in Column A have not been listed in the right order. Put them in the correct order and match them with the dates on which they occurred in Column B. Scanning the story of the Basotho for these dates will help you to do this exercise.

Scanning means reading very quickly to find specific information. When you scan you don't read all the words on the page. You let your eye move quickly over the page until the information you want catches your eye.

Column A	Column B
The Napier treaty was signed which established the boundaries of the Basotho kingdom for the first time.	1868
A British army, supported by the Griqua, Kora, Rolong and some Boers was defeated by the Basotho.	1835
The Great Trek started.	1843
The OFS declared war on the Basotho kingdom and was defeated by them.	1851
Land wars caused a great upheaval in southern Africa.	1854
The Bloemfontein Convention was held which gave rise to the OFS.	1858
The British agreed to take over the Basotho kingdom and it became known as "Basutoland".	1865
The War of Cannon's Boom broke out between the OFS and the Basotho.	1820s and 1830s

UNIT 8

Exercise 8

Timelines are a useful way of summarising and making clearer the order in which events took place and the length of time between events. Draw a timeline showing all the incidents that were mentioned in the previous exercise.

> **HOW TO DRAW A TIMELINE**
>
> 1. Decide what length you want your timeline to be. This means you have to work out a scale. Remember that the information that your timeline shows must be easy to read. Your timeline needs to cover a period of about fifty years — from 1820 to 1870.
>
> 2. Fill in the dates which mark your scale on the left-hand side of the timeline. Starting from the bottom, work your way up from the past into the present. Then plot the dates of the important events on the right-hand side.
>
> 3. Write a short description of the event next to each date on the right-hand side.
>
> 4. Give your timeline a title.

How much land did the Basotho lose?

Just as a matter of interest, let's work out approximately how much land the Basotho lost from 1843 to 1868.

Exercise 9

What percentage of the land given to them at the time of the Napier treaty had the Basotho lost by the time the British took over the area and called it "Basutoland"?

Work out how much land the Basotho lost by using the following maps:

Napier Boundary page 115

Basutoland page 121

> **HOW TO ESTIMATE THE AREA OF A COUNTRY OR PIECE OF LAND FROM A MAP**
>
> 1. Examine the scale at the bottom of the map. It looks like this:
>
>   0 10 20 30 40 km
>
>   The numbers will change from one map to the next. This is because different maps have different scales. (Note: The two maps you are working with have the same scale.) They tell you what distances in the real world are represented by distances on the map.

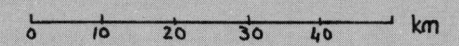

UNIT 8

2. Get hold of a piece of tracing paper large enough to cover the maps you are working with. Draw a grid of one centimetre squares i.e. each side of each square must be one centimetre long.

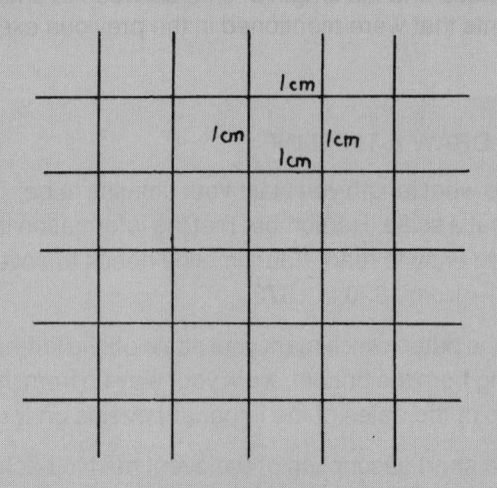

1cm : 10km

3. From the line scale on your map, work out how many kilometres one centimetre represents. In the example above, the scale is 1cm : 10 km. Using this scale, one square on the grid would represent 100 square kilometres.

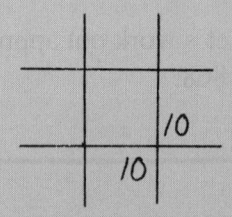

i.e. 10 km x 10 km = 100 km^2

4. Place your tracing paper grid over the map or piece of land that you want to estimate the area for. Make sure that the border or limit of your land area is visible through the tracing paper.

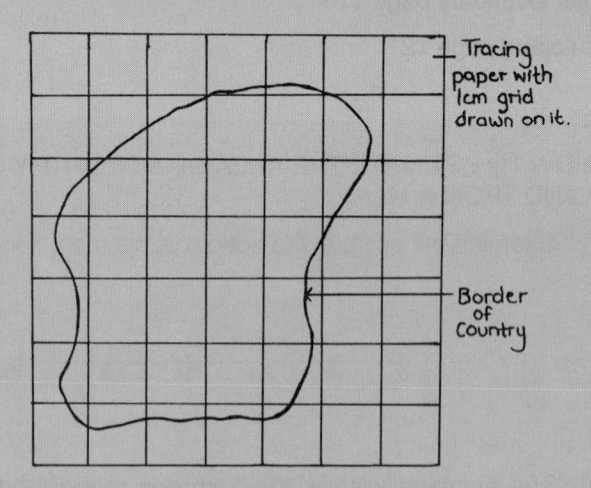

5. Count the number of whole squares that fall within the border. These are the ones that are not "cut off" by the border. Write this number down. In the example above, there are 14.

6. Now count the number of squares that have part of their area "cut off" by the border. Write this number down. Now divide this number by two. (In the above example, there are 20 part squares, divided by two, gives you 10.)

7. Add the number of whole squares to the number of part squares divided by two i.e. 14 + 10. This represents an estimate of the number of square units covered by the map. To work out the area in kilometres, you simply convert this number using your scale. (In the example, the number of square units covered by the map is 24. If one unit is 100 square kilometres, then the map would cover approximately 24 × 100 i.e. 2 400 square kilometres.

Note: The final figure is only an estimated area but for purposes of comparing size it is quite accurate. If you want a more accurate estimation of land area, you need to take factors like mountains and valleys into consideration.

Something to think about

Some people say that Moshoeshoe saved Lesotho from becoming part of South Africa with all its apartheid laws. Other people say that it has made little difference. After Moshoeshoe's death, Lesotho became much poorer. Having lost so much farming land, the Basotho were forced to farm land that wouldn't normally be used every year. This led to overgrazing and erosion.

Eroded land is a common sight in Lesotho today

Because people were no longer able to survive on the land, they were forced to become migrant labourers in the mines of South Africa. And today, although Lesotho is independent politically, it remains dependent on South Africa economically.

UNIT 8

With all the changes that have been happening, do you think that Lesotho should become part of South Africa? Should the government give back the land which, to begin with, was used by the Basotho? Or should Lesotho remain as it is today?

Summing up

The main ideas that have been covered in this unit are:

1. By 1840, Moshoeshoe had managed to build a strong Basotho state which included what is today part of the Orange Free State as well as Lesotho. Moshoeshoe's territory was recognised by the Napier Treaty of 1843.

2. To avoid conflict with the Boers, Moshoeshoe agreed to make a section of the Caledon River Valley available to the Boers.

3. In 1848, Sir Harry Smith proclaimed British control over the Basotho territory.

4. At the Bloemfontein Convention in 1854, the British recognised the independence of the Boers in the area between the Orange and the Vaal. This became the Orange Free State.

5. After this, wars broke out between the OFS and the Basotho Kingdom. Moshoeshoe could not go on and on fighting the Boers so he eventually appealed to the British to take over the Basotho Kingdom.

6. When this happened in 1869, the Basotho Kingdom became known as "Basutoland" and the Basotho people became British subjects. The Basotho people lost about one third of their land to the Boers. This happened to be their most fertile land.

Having land was very important as it provided people with the means of feeding themselves and their families. It also gave people the option of growing crops and rearing livestock which they could sell. The last unit examines how people are affected when they lose their land.

UNIT 9

"We who were first, have come to be last"

UNIT 9

"We who were first, have come to be last"

By the end of the 19th Century, the Khoisan had lost their land and no independent African kingdoms existed. The Boers had set up republics in the OFS and the Transvaal, while the British had control of the Cape Colony and Natal. This brought the establishment of a central government in southern Africa a step closer. The major battle for power was now between the Boers and the British.

The British finally defeated the Boers in the Anglo-Boer War which ended in 1902. Then in 1910, without consulting any African people, the British gave the Boers the right to govern the whole country. This was similar to what happened when the British gave the Boers the right to rule over areas in which the Basotho had been living.

In 1913, the Land Act was passed. By law, Africans could not own land in 87% of the country. A process of removing people from the land of their forefathers started. This process has continued until very recently.

Let's look at what has become of the !Kung, the first community we studied in this book. Their story is but one of a thousand that could be told by the people of South Africa. It is the story about the effects on a community of losing its land.

Looking at the changes that have taken place for the !Kung and other San groups will give you an idea of the powerful connection between the past and the present. It will show you what happens to a society that is forced to change its way of life. You will see what happens when the "strings" that connect people in a community to the land and to one another are "broken".

Changes experienced by the !Kung

The photographs that follow will show you some of the changes experienced by the !Kung of Nyae Nyae over the last 30 years.

Exercise 1

Divide into groups of four.

Look at these photographs of the !Kung and read the captions. They were taken by Paul Weinberg in 1989 in what was the Nyae Nyae district. Then discuss these questions in your groups.

1. What has changed for the !Kung?
2. What things have remained the same?
3. Why do you think these changes have taken place?

UNIT 9

Playing the dongu

Tsumkwe

UNIT 9

Cattle farming

Dancing the Melon Dance, Gairna School, Gobabis

UNIT 9

Prayer parade

Week-end festivities, Tsumkwe

UNIT 9

In the past 40 years, life has changed drastically for the !Kung. The information below points out the main **causes** of change and what the **effects** of it have been.

Exercise 2

Your teacher will read this information to the whole class. As you are following in your own book, notice the **causes** of the changes that the !Kung have experienced.

Shaken roots

Namibia, or South West Africa as it was then called, became a "protectorate" of the South African government in 1921. This was an arrangement made after the First World War. German colonies were handed over to the countries who won the war. This meant that South West Africa was to be ruled by the South African government.

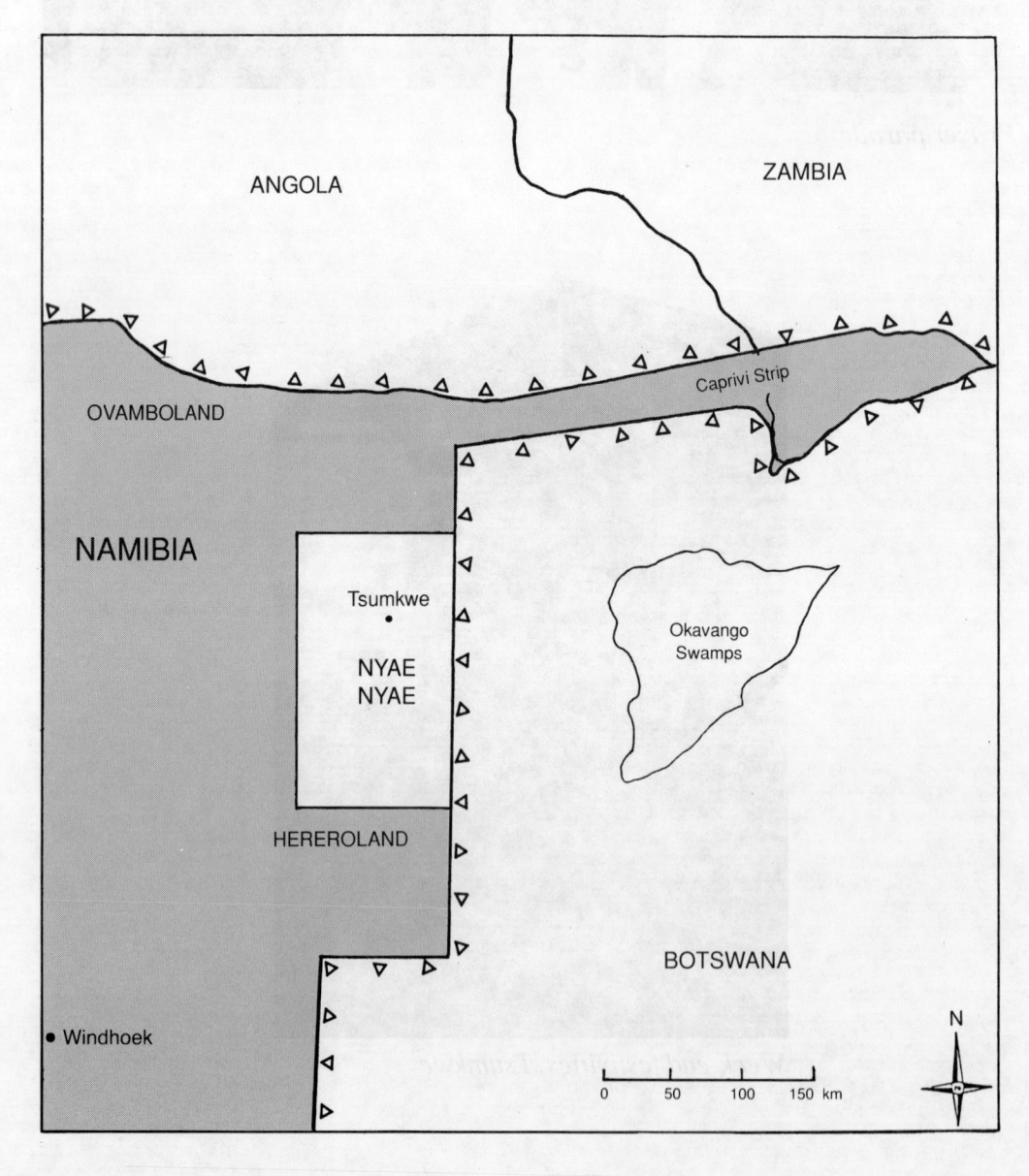

132

UNIT 9

① In 1960 a government post was established at a place in the Nyae Nyae district called Tsumkwe (see map on the previous page). All the !Kung bands together with groups of San people from other parts of Namibia, were assembled at Tsumkwe. They were given a school, a clinic, a church, a large jail and some jobs. Some men were employed to build roads and to be house servants. In this way, these San people began to earn small amounts of money and to be involved in a new form of economic exchange: working for money and using this money to buy what they needed. Though most bands still continued to hunt and gather, living at the government post brought great changes to their lives.

Poisoning arrows

UNIT 9

② The main reason about 1 000 people came to live at Tsumkwe was because the administration promised to teach them gardening and the raising of goats. In this way, an area which had once supported only about 25 people by hunting and gathering quickly became overcrowded.

Kxao/Ai!ae at work in his garden

Also, a government-subsidised bottle-store was added to the Tsumkwe store. In time, drinking became a community problem. People drink when they feel despair about their lives. They lose their pride when they have no work and are unable to provide for their families. Drinking makes them forget their problems.

As Dabe Dahm, a member of the Tsumkwe community put it at a meeting to discuss the problem, "When you drink, you shouldn't go around thinking like a Boer and telling people that you are a big shot. If you do that, someday people will become angry with you and their hearts will grow big against you . . . So, when we drink, let's not fight. Let's start to talk to each other about drinking and help each other."

To make matters worse, the local bush foods disappeared fast because of the demands of such a large settlement on the resources in the area. This, together with the problem of increasing unemployment and heavy drinking, had the effect of turning Tsumkwe into a rural slum. It became known as "the place of death".

③ In 1970 the government established Bushmanland for the San. The Nyae Nyae area, where the !Kung had lived for so long, had never been "given" to them by the government as a homeland or in any other way. In establishing Bushmanland, the government divided the Nyae Nyae area into three parts. Only one third of the Nyae Nyae district became Bushmanland. They made the northern part a trophy-hunting game reserve. They gave the southern part to the Herero, traditional cattle-farmers who make up about one third of the population of Namibia. Many areas that had previously provided the !Kung with important sources of water and food were not included in the area they were given.

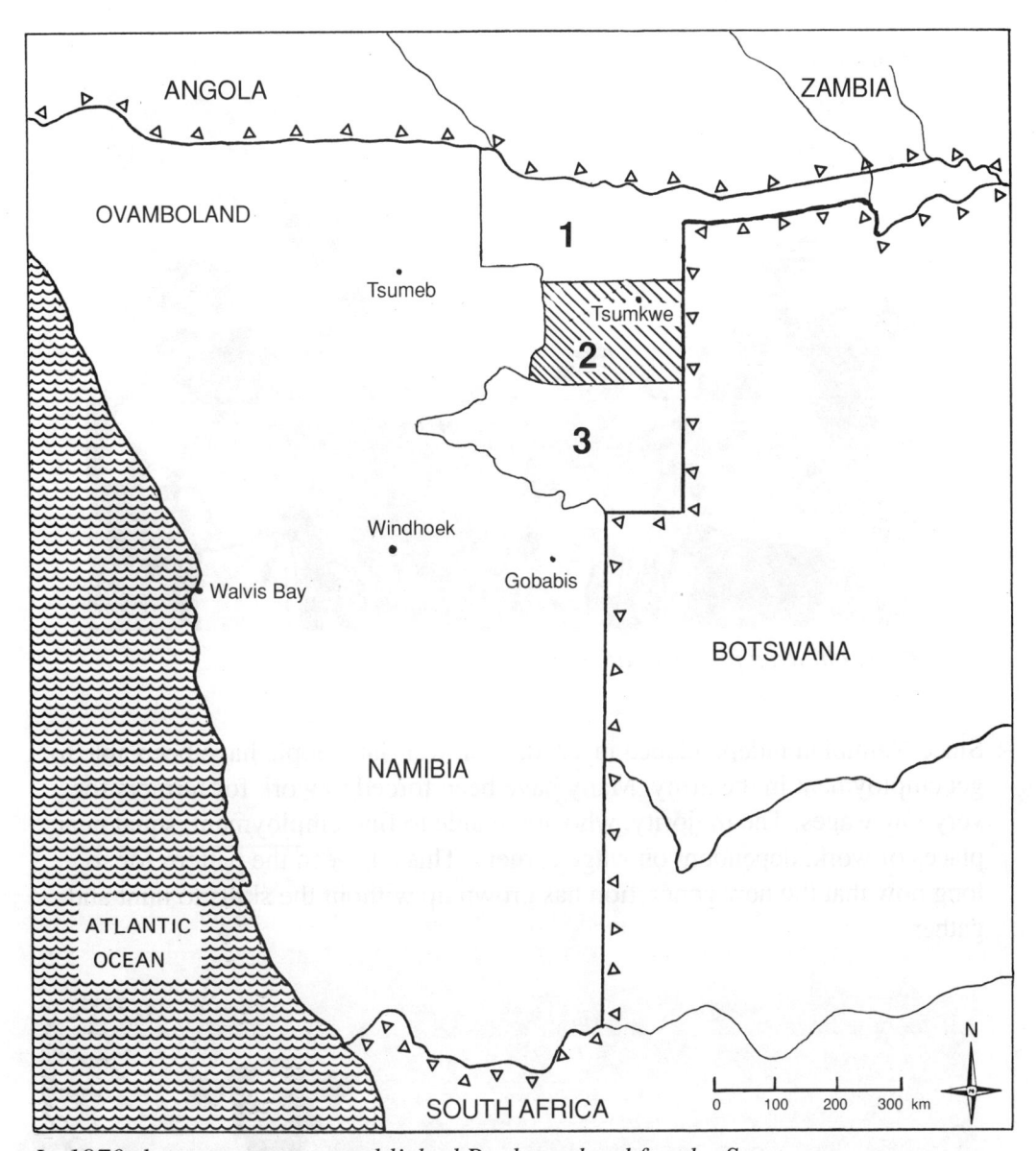

UNIT 9

In 1970 the government established Bushmanland for the San

During the course of the Namibian struggle for independence, the South African army recruited the San in the war against Swapo*. The South African army took advantage of the tracking skills of the San and encouraged them to think of Swapo as "the enemy". When Bushmanland was established, the army dug very deep boreholes in the driest part and set up army posts there. The !Kung as well as San people from other parts of Namibia who became soldiers were stationed at these posts.

As a !Kung woman called #Toma said:

The South African soldiers will bring fighting here. We're good people. We'd share the pot with Swapo. But these soldiers are the owners of fighting. They fight even when they play, and I fear them. I won't let my children be soldiers, the experts of anger.

135

UNIT 9

!Kung children playing cadets

⑤ Since Namibian independence in 1990, far fewer San people have been able to get employment in the army. Many have been forced to work for farmers for very low wages. The majority, who are unable to find employment, squat near places of work, dependent on wage earners. This has been the pattern for so long now that the new generation has grown up without the skills to hunt and gather.

A Herero woman and the San family that works for her

Agerob and Mr Hentjie Barnard on his farm, Gobabis

Today 33 000 San people in Namibia have hardly any land on which to live. This means they cannot hunt, gather or produce their own food and they are increasingly without work.

For some, the setting up of the Nyae Nyae Farmers' Co-operative in 1989 has made life a bit easier. The San in Bushmanland know they do not have enough land to be able to survive on hunting and gathering alone. So, they have started a new life as farmers. They have small herds of cattle which the Co-operative has helped them to obtain and they are planting gardens. Life is not easy and they struggle against many things: against lions that kill their cattle; against elephants that trample their gardens and wreck their water pumps and against unhelpful or hostile officials who believe that they are incapable of changing their ways.

In the middle of 1989, the United Nations started a process of teaching people about elections* so that they would know how to vote for a new government. Before this, the Farmers' Co-op in Bushmanland tried to explain elections to people who had no word for them in their language. For people who claimed,

UNIT 9

"We have no headman, each one of us is headman over himself", it was difficult to understand the need to choose leaders to represent their community in the new politics.

"An election means to come to an understanding about your n!ore."

"An election means that you give praise to the person who will sit in the chair of leading, the head person."

Discussing the elections

The inhabitants of Bushmanland did vote in the national election in 1989. The UN sent a helicopter with a voting booth from water hole to water hole!

One of the things the San believe is that their old N!ore system could form the basis of the new land laws of the country. In N!ore law, every person has the right of residence. People inherit the right to live permanently in an area from their mothers and fathers. "Where your mother and father are buried is where you have your strength," they say. The San know this system of land rights has been successful over a long span of time. They believe it could be their special contribution towards nation-building.

At present, the people of Bushmanland are still hoping to have the land on which they live recognised by the government as belonging to them in some way. This has not happened as yet.

UNIT 9

> **New words**

- Swapo — South West African People's Organisation, the liberation movement which fought for 30 years for Namibian independence from South African control. In November 1989, Swapo won the election and now governs an independent Namibia.
- UN election information process — the UN set up UNTAG in Namibia to keep peace over the time of the elections for a new government for an independent Namibia. They had to ensure that the elections were free and fair. Part of their job was to inform people about what the different political parties stood for so that people understood what they were voting for.

*The place does not feel to me
as the place used to feel.
The place does not feel pleasant to me
because the string has broken for me.*

Ranking the causes

There are often many causes for a particular situation but one or two may be more important than the others.

Exercise 3

Do this exercise with a partner.

1. Together, make a list of all the causes you can find for changes amongst the !Kung.

UNIT 9

2. Now rank these causes starting with the one you think is the most important and ending with the one you think is least important. If you think two causes are equally important, put them next to each other.

1. _____
2. _____   2. _____   (if, for example, you think these 2 causes are equally important)
3. _____
4. _____

Thinking about the future

The story of the !Kung shows us what happens to a community when it loses its n!ore — when it has no place that it can call its own. This is the fate that millions of South Africans have faced over the last two centuries — and especially through forced removals over the last 40 years. But this could be the subject of another whole book.

Do this last exercise to round off what you have learned in this book.

Exercise 4

140

UNIT 9

Work with a partner.

The government in South Africa, like the Namibian government, will have to make new laws about the way land is to be divided among all the people who live here.

Write a letter to **Upbeat** magazine in which you express your views about how land was divided in the past. Suggest how we can learn from the past so that we don't make the same mistakes in the future.

Upbeat is a magazine for teenagers which likes to publish the views of teenagers about current affairs.

Stage 1

Before you start writing ....

We have seen from our study of the !Kung that what happened in the past has a direct effect on the present. So, before you start writing, refresh your memory about what happened in the past:

- Read and discuss the table you completed at the end of Unit 7, which summarises the attitudes to land of all the people who were living in South Africa by the beginning of the 19th Century.
- Read and talk to each other about Unit 8 which examines aspects of the conflict over land in the 19th Century.
- Read the ideas of the San in Namibia about the sharing of land in the future.

Stage 2

Organise your letter to the editor of **Upbeat** like this:

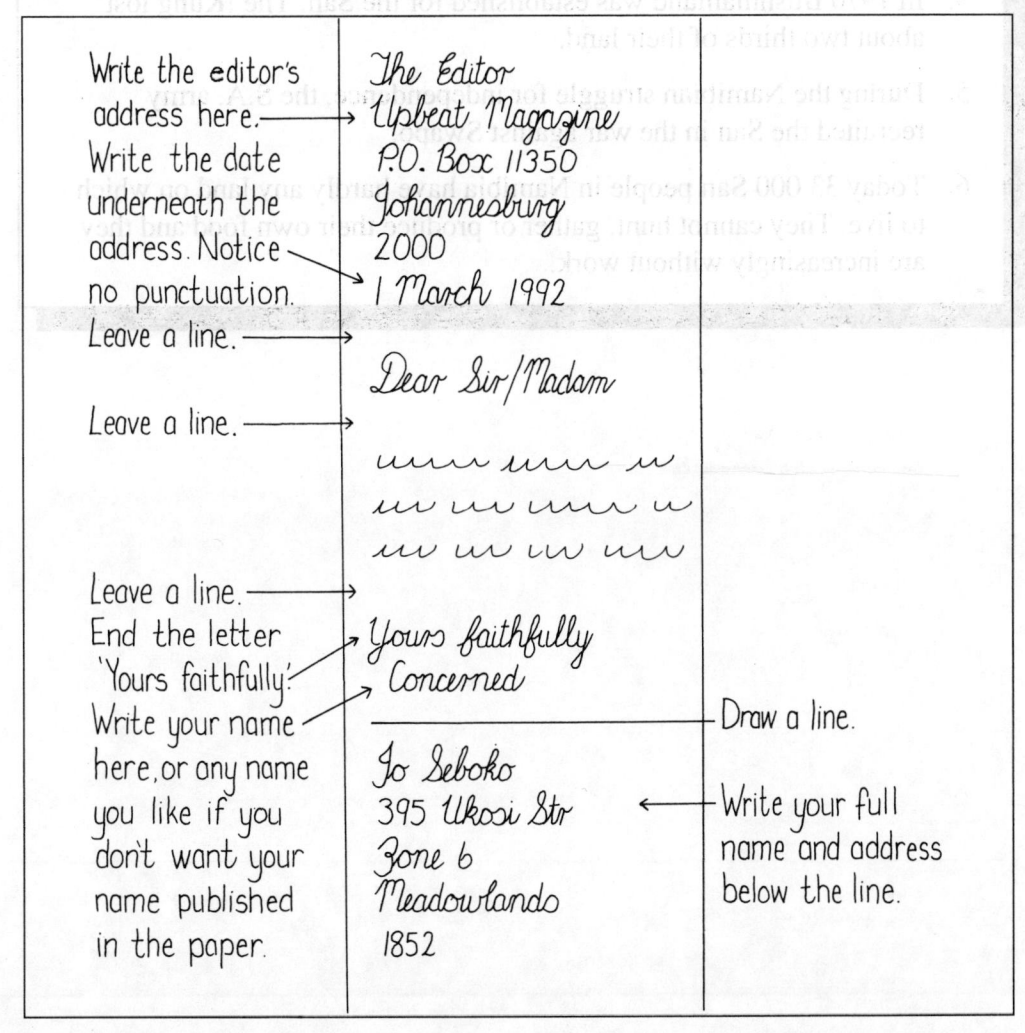

Write the editor's address here. Write the date underneath the address. Notice no punctuation.	The Editor Upbeat Magazine P.O. Box 11350 Johannesburg 2000 1 March 1992	
Leave a line.		
	Dear Sir/Madam	
Leave a line.		
	~~ ~~~~ ~~ ~~ ~~ ~~~~ ~~ ~~ ~~ ~~ ~~~	
Leave a line. End the letter 'Yours faithfully'. Write your name here, or any name you like if you don't want your name published in the paper.	Yours faithfully Concerned ───────── Jo Seboko 395 Ukosi Str Zone 6 Meadowlands 1852	Draw a line. Write your full name and address below the line.

141

UNIT 9

Once your letter has been corrected and you have had the chance to rework it, why not post it to **Upbeat** magazine? The address is in the box above which shows you how to set out your letter. You never know — it could get published!

Summing up

The main ideas you learned about in this unit are listed below:

1. Over the last 30 years, the !Kung of Nyae Nyae have experienced great changes.

2. These changes were caused by the establishment of a government post at Tsumkwe in 1960. This involved the San people in a new form of economic exchange: working for money and using this money to buy what they needed.

3. Problems that arose included the following:
   - drinking became a community problem
   - local bush foods disappeared because too many people were living in one area
   - unemployment increased.

4. In 1970 Bushmanland was established for the San. The !Kung lost about two thirds of their land.

5. During the Namibian struggle for independence, the S.A. army recruited the San in the war against Swapo.

6. Today 33 000 San people in Namibia have hardly any land on which to live. They cannot hunt, gather or produce their own food and they are increasingly without work.

BIBLIOGRAPHY

The references used in the research for this book have been grouped to correspond with the nine units of the book.

UNIT 1: THE ORIGIN OF PEOPLE and

UNIT 2: ARCHAEOLOGY — A WAY OF REDISCOVERING THE PAST

    Cameron, T and Spies, S B (eds): *An Illustrated History of South Africa*, Jonathan Ball, Johannesburg, 1986.

    Mason, R: *Origins of the African People of the Johannesburg Area*, Skotaville, Johannesburg, 1987.

    Muller, J: "Culture, Society and Education in South Africa" in Tomaselli, K (ed): *Rethinking Culture*, Anthropos Publishers, Bellville, 1988.

    Seidman, J: *In Our Own Image*, Foundation for Education with Production (FEP), Gaberone, 1990.

    Thackeray, A I et al: *The Early History of Southern Africa to AD 1500*, College Tutorial Press, Cape Town, 1990.

    Witz, L: *Write Your Own History*, Sached/Ravan, Johannesburg, 1988.

    Yates, R and Parkington, J and Manhire, T: *Pictures from the Past*, Centaur Publications, Pietermaritzburg, 1990.

UNIT 3: HUNTER-GATHERERS IN SOUTHERN AFRICA

    Biesele, M and Weinberg, P: *Shaken Roots —The Bushmen of Namibia*, EDA Publications, Johannesburg, 1990.

    Bleek, W H I and Lloyd, L C: *Specimens of Bushmen Folklore*, George Allen, London, 1911.

    Lee, R B: *The Dobe !Kung*, Holt, Rinehart and Winston, London, 1984.

    Lee, R B: *The !Kung San: Men, Women and Work in a Foraging Society*, Cambridge University Press, Cambridge, 1979.

    Lee, R B and De Vore, I (eds): *Kalahari Hunter-Gatherers*, Harvard University Press, Cambridge, Massachusetts, 1978.

    Malherbe, C: *These Small People*, Shuter & Shooter, Pietermaritzburg, 1983.

    Marshall, L: *The !Kung of Nyae Nyae*, Harvard University Press, Cambridge, Massachusetts, 1976.

UNIT 4: THE ARRIVAL OF THE KHOIKHOI

    Balkema, A A (ed): *Jan van Riebeeck Journal*, Vol 3, 1659 - 1662, Balkema, Cape Town, 1958.

    Hiscock, D: *Assessment and the History Curriculum Development: Report on a visit to the UK, April - May 1990*. Unpublished.

    Kennedy, R F (ed): *Africana Museum Catalogue of Prints*, Vol 1 & 2, Johannesburg Africana Museum, 1975.

    Kolb, P: *The Present State of the Cape of Good Hope*, London, 1738.

    Malherbe, C: *Men of Men*, Shuter & Shooter, Pietermaritzburg, 1983.

    Nisbet, J et al: *History Alive—Std 5*, Shuter & Shooter, Pietermaritzburg, 1985.

    Raper, R and Boucher, M (eds): *Travels of Colonel Robert Gordon*, Vol 1 & 2, Brenthurst Press, Johannesburg, 1988.

Raven-Hart, R (ed): *Before van Riebeeck, Callers at South Africa from 1488 to 1652,* Struik reprint, Cape Town, 1967.

Raven-Hart, R (ed): *Cape of Good Hope, 1652 - 1707, The first fifty years of Dutch colonisation as seen by callers,* Balkema, Cape Town, 1971.

Saunders, C and Bundy, C (eds): *Illustrated History of South Africa, The Real Story,* Reader's Digest Association South Africa, Cape Town, 1988.

S.A. Library Quarterly Bulletin, December 1988.

UNIT 5: AFRICAN FARMERS IN SOUTHERN AFRICA

Malherbe, C and Hall, M: *Changing the Land,* Shuter & Shooter, Pietermaritzburg, 1988.

Miller, P: *Myths and Legends of Southern Africa,* T.V. Bulpin Publications, Cape Town, 1979.

Nisbet, J et al: *History Alive — Std 6,* Shuter & Shooter, Pietermaritzburg, 1985.

Scott, J (ed): *Understanding Cause and Effect,* Teaching History Research Group, Longman, London, 1990.

West, M: *Abantu: An Introduction to the Black People of South Africa,* Struik, Cape Town, 1976.

UNIT 6: THE STRUGGLE OVER LAND

Bundy, C: *Re-making the Past, New Perspectives in South African History,* Dept. of Adult Education and Extra-mural Studies, UCT, 1986.

Elphick, R: *Khoikhoi and the Founding of White South Africa,* Ravan, Johannesburg, 1985.

Hiscock, D: *The Aboriginal Peoples of the Cape.* Unpublished.

Lomas, T: *Empathy: Teaching, Learning and Assessing.* Unpublished.

Press, K: *Krotoa,* Centaur Publications, Pietermaritzburg, 1990.

Saunders, C: *The Making of the South African Past,* David Philip, Cape Town, 1988.

SERB (Southern Regional Examinations Board): *Empathy in History: From Definition to Assessment,* The Southern Regional Examination Board, Southampton, 1986.

UNIT 7: THE STRUGGLE OVER LAND

Elphick, R and Giliomee, H (eds): *The Shaping of South African Society, 1652 - 1840,* Maskew Miller Longman, Cape Town, 1989.

James, W and Simons, M (eds): *The Angry Divide,* David Philip, Johannesburg, 1989.

Malherbe, C and Saunders, C: *Struggle for the Land,* Shuter & Shooter, Pietermaritzburg, 1990.

Lamar, H and Thompson, L (eds): *The Frontier in History: North America and Southern Africa compared,* Yale University Press, New Haven, 1981.

Lategan, F V: *Die Boer se Roer,* Sentrale Pers, Bloemfontein, 1967.

The Trading Game, Christian Aid, London, 1986.

Versfeld, R: *Sowing and Harvesting,* Oxfam Publication, Oxford, 1989.

UNIT 8: THE STRUGGLE OVER LAND

Lambrechts, H and Smit, G J J: *New History for Std 6,* Nasou Limited, Cape Town, 1979.

Sached: *The Land the Basotho lost,* Sached/Centaur Publications, Pietermaritzburg, 1992.

Sanders, P: *Moshoeshoe — Chief of the Sotho,* Heinemann, London, 1975.

Thompson, L: *Survival in Two Worlds: Moshoeshoe of Lesotho*, Oxford University Press, London, 1975.

UNIT 9: WE WHO WERE FIRST, HAVE COME TO BE LAST

Biesele, M and Weinberg, P: *Shaken Roots - The Bushmen of Namibia*, EDA Publications, Johannesburg, 1990.

Development Education Centre: *Theme work: Approaches for Teaching with a Global Perspective*, Birmingham, 1986.

Marshall, L: *Notes on Changes experienced by the Nyae Nyae !Kung*. Unpublished.

Learn and Teach, Number 4, 1989: *Vote Swapo for Freedom*.

Learn and Teach, Number 3, 1990: *Namibia: The Birth of a Nation*.

ACKNOWLEDGEMENTS

Page 8 —*Four Million Years of Hominid Evolution*, Stream Education Movement, Retreat, 1990. Page 14 — Seidman, J: *In Our Own Image*, Foundation for Education with Production, Gaberone, 1990. Pages 41-42 — Biesele, M: "Aspects of !Kung Folklore" in Lee, R B and De Vore, I (eds): *Kalahari Hunter-Gatherers*, Harvard University Press, Cambridge, Massachusetts, 1978. Pages 47-52 — Malherbe, C: *Men of Men* (1983). Pages 49-50 — Nisbet, J *et al*: *History Alive — Std 5* (1984), Shuter and Shooter, Pietermaritzburg. Pages 54-55 — *Illustrated History of South Africa: The Real Story*, Reader's Digest Association South Africa, Cape Town, 1988.

Photographs/illustrations

Paul Weinberg, SouthLight, front and back cover, pages 129-131, 133-134, 136-139.
The Star, page 3.
Richard Lee, page 37.
Lorna Marshall, all photographs of the !Kung in Unit 3 except Richard Lee, page 37.
Africana Museum, pages 50, 83, 85, 89, 93, 96, 99, 101, 109, 111, 113, 116, 118 (top left), 120.
S.A. Library, pages 75, 78.
Cape Times, 1985, Grogan cartoon, page 86.
National Museum, page 117.
Cape Archives, page 118 (bottom left)
B. Woodhouse, private collection, pages 114, 125.
A. Zieminski and The Sached Trust, page 140.
Prof. R. Mason and Skotaville Publishers, illustrations in Unit 5 — redrawn from illustrations created for the book *Origins of the African People of the Johannesburg Area*, 1987.

The publishers have made every effort to trace Copyright holders. However, we shall be very glad to hear from anyone who has been inadvertently overlooked or incorrectly cited and make the necessary changes at the first opportunity.